ANDY PETTITTE
& BOB RECCORD WITH MARK TABB

TruthQuest

STRIKE ZONE

TARGETING A LIFE OF
**INTEGRITY
& PURITY**

GENERAL EDITOR:
STEVE KEELS

BROADMAN
& HOLMAN
PUBLISHERS

NASHVILLE, TENNESSEE

10-digit ISBN: 0805430873
13-digit ISBN: 9780805430875

Published by Broadman & Holman Publishers,
Nashville, Tennessee

Dewey Decimal Classification: 248.82
Subject Headings: BOYS—RELIGIOUS LIFE
CHRISTIAN LIFE
PURITY (ETHICS)

Unless otherwise noted, all quotes are from the Holman Christian Standard Bible. © 1999, 2000, 2002, Holman Bible Publishers. Quotations marked NIV are taken from the Holy Bible, New International Version, © 1973, 1978, and 1984 The International Bible Society, used by permission of Zondervan Publishing House, all rights reserved; and NKJV, the New King James Version, © 1979, 1980, 1982, Thomas Nelson, Inc., Publishers.

1 2 3 4 5 6 7 8 9 10 09 08 07 06 05

FROM ANDY:

To Laura, Josh, Jared, and Lexy.
I pray I can continue to be a man of integrity and
character for you. I hope I will always be the Christian
husband and father I know the Lord wants from me.

FROM BOB:

To my son Bryan of whom I am proud beyond words.
You have traveled through the teen years and entered
adulthood as a man of integrity, character, and humor.
And you're a man I have a blast sharing life with!
Thanks for making life count!

Contents

Charting a Path toward Purity

CHAPTER ONE

Beware of the Minefields

BOB

The smell of gunfire hung in the air like a heavy blanket. The jungle humidity seemed so thick that a knife wouldn't cut through it. Men dripped with sweat caused by a combination of the jungle heat and fear. At any moment bullets might start flying like swarming bees.

It was Easter morning on Thunder Road, one of the most fought-over pieces of turf in the Vietnam War. The American troops on maneuvers trying to root out the Vietcong paused just long enough to celebrate the holiday. They felt a world away from the traditions with which many of them had grown up. Back in the States this Sunday morning was probably a beautiful day. Families drifted to churches to celebrate the resurrection of Jesus Christ. Hymns were sung and stirring messages preached proclaiming the highest of Christian holidays. After church, family after family gathered around a table with the smell of home-cooked meals filling the air. Laughter bounced off the walls of dining rooms, followed by Easter egg hunts for the children in the yard.

Egg hunts and laughter were a long way away from the intense firefight exploding around the soldiers on Thunder Road. But one man seemed out of place. Missionary Jim Humphries stood with the soldiers. He came to bring them a note of hope from the Word of God. He knew every man in front of him faced death every minute of every day. But they were here serving their country, fighting for freedom, and putting their lives on the line even for those back home who didn't appreciate it.

As the soldiers focused on Jim's message, the enemy focused on the worshipping soldiers and, suddenly, opened fire. Instinctively the American troops scattered for cover. Drawing on their training and experience in jungle warfare, each soldier knew exactly what to do. But not the missionary. Not knowing where else to go, Jim took off running down a side trail. He didn't pay attention whether soldiers were with him because he had one overwhelming desire—to get away from the gun fire, find a safe place, and hide until it was over. The firefight seemed to last an eternity. In reality it was only a few minutes, but when your life's on the line, minutes turn into hours.

The explosion of shells was over as fast as it began. Suddenly a voice shouted, "Preacher! Stop where you are! Don't take another step or you're dead!" Freezing in place, Jim Humphries came to a halt and looked around. Behind him he saw two soldiers who had fled after him. Unlike Jim, they hadn't been searching for a place to hide from the battle. No, they had tried in vain to stop him. He was headed into an enemy minefield.

The lieutenant in charge came running up to the edge of the minefield. Amazed that neither Humphries nor the two soldiers had inadvertently stepped on a mine and been blown into the next century, he quickly surveyed the scene. He could tell Humphries was scared stiff and that the soldiers who'd tried to help him had stepped directly into harm's way. Trying to sound calm, the lieutenant quickly explained that one false step could kill all three of them. "You guys need to stand frozen until someone can walk in there and get you out." He then turned to the rest of his platoon and said, "Any volunteers?"

As luck would have it, a soldier from Tennessee with a size 13 boot volunteered. Everybody else froze. The lieutenant probably thought to himself, *Why couldn't someone with a size 6 or 7 foot have volunteered? After all, this is a minefield!* Reluctantly, he gave his approval because nobody else was rushing to the front for the job. Carefully, patiently, while everyone else held his breath, the big-footed soldier from Tennessee made his way to the stranded threesome. Feeling his way with a knife and taking very careful steps with those size 13 feet, it took him almost an hour to cover the distance of about fifteen to twenty yards to the three stranded men. As he arrived everybody breathed easier. Then came his profound instructions, "I'm going to turn around and lead you out of here. Make sure your footsteps fall in my footprints. If they don't, you may blow up all four of us. Pay attention. Every step you take will mean your life and mine!"

Slowly, he pivoted and began to make his way back. Missionary Jim Humphries and the two soldiers followed. Each one placed his feet carefully within the big guy's footprints. And it saved their lives that hot, humid Easter on Thunder Road!

Minefields of Life

Today, the world in which you live is also filled with minefields. As a young man charting your course through life, you've seen for yourself it's a dangerous walk. You vow to demonstrate moral leadership, but the guys in the locker room are brutal when you don't laugh at their coarse humor. You pledge to be pure, but your buddy clicks on a link and hard-core porn pops on the computer screen. You avoid temptation, but your girlfriend shows up in *that* outfit. *She could have gone all year without wearing that,* you think. And you get frustrated with yourself for staring . . . and thinking . . . !

The Christian journey can be both exhilarating at times and absolutely unnerving. One false step could bring tragic results. Your good intentions blow up. So does your testimony. That's why God loves you enough to have sent a guide to walk you out of the minefield of life and make sure you negotiate the journey safely.

The guide's name is Jesus Christ.

He calls you to follow Him through the treacherous terrain of life. He begs you to make sure that your footsteps fall in His footprints. You can find them in His book of promises to you, the Bible. He won't *make* you follow Him. The decision is yours. You can follow His guidance or you can go your own way. Your careful attention to those footprints and to His instruction can make all the difference in how you come through.

You've already discovered that minefields are scattered everywhere. A prom party turns wild. A friend tempts you to cheat. A date tests your resolve to wait until marriage. False steps in any direction can leave you wounded, hurting, critically injured. Sometimes the pain is physical and other times emotional or spiritual . . . and still other times all three at once. A lot of life's minefields start out as dangerous attitudes and just plain lies. Do these sound familiar?

Minefield 1: Truth Is Relative, and Nothing Is Absolute

There's a growing trend to claim that truth is not an absolute standard given by Almighty God which is true for everyone, in all places and at all times. Instead, according to some people, truth is what my experience or circumstances tell me it ought to be. They say each one of us has the ability to make up our own standard of truth which is "flexible" according to whatever circumstances we face.

Several years ago, a professor at a leading university wrote *The Closing of the American Mind*, a book on his observations of new university students. He found very few, including those who grew up in church, who believed that truth is absolute. Almost all saw right and wrong, true and false, as relative to the situation.

My friend, Josh McDowell, in doing research for his book *Right from Wrong*, discovered that 57 percent of junior and senior high school students do not believe in an objective, absolute standard of truth. He also found that 85 percent of students who attend church on a regular basis agree with this statement: "What is right for one person in a given situation might not be right for another person who encounters the same situation."

George Barna, who leads an organization that studies trends throughout America both inside and outside the church, goes one step further. He found that 80 percent of those between the ages of twelve and twenty reject the concept of absolute truth. Here's what he said: "The spirituality of Americans is Christian in name only. We desire experience more than knowledge. We prefer choices to absolutes. We embrace preferences rather than truths. We seek comfort rather than growth. Faith must come on our terms or we reject it. We have enthroned ourselves as the final arbiters of righteousness, the ultimate rulers of our own experience and destiny."[1]

But, if there's no absolute truth, what standard do you have to make good decisions? The absence of truth means there's no footprint you can trust to put your own footsteps in. You're left stranded, frozen, in the middle of the minefield.

Minefield 2: If You Really Care for Each Other, What's the Big Deal about Sex?

Our culture says, "If it feels good, do it." Many guys think, *If the opportunity for sex presents itself, why walk away? I might miss something good! And besides that, everybody else is doing it.* The message comes at us from everywhere. Stars from the music and movie industries make it pretty clear that you don't have to get tied down with commitment to have a good time. Yet this idea leaves lives crashed and burning on the ground when the "good time" is over.

And just so we're clear on the extreme danger of this minefield, let's be sure we're really aware of just how dangerous, and tricky, this minefield can be. A lot of guys—even the ones who sit in church on Sunday and attend FCA Huddles, Young Life, or other campus-focused activities Monday through Friday—have figured that they can compartmentalize their lives. In other words, whatever happens on dates or messing around at parties doesn't affect their "church" life. They can be kept in different worlds. And as long as things stop short of intercourse, it's really not sex anyway!

An interesting thought . . . but wrong! Jesus said our thoughts alone can get us in a lot of trouble. In Matthew 5:27–28 He says that if I undress a girl in the privacy of my thought world and fantasize intimate acts with her I'm as guilty as if I had done it in the flesh. The Bible says that while others may simply see our action, God sees what is the real deal in our hearts. And that's tough when the average age of introduction to pornography today is eleven![2]

And get this. The word that is used for "immorality" throughout the New Testament is a word that covers a vast range of sexual activity outside of marriage including wandering hands under a girls clothes, genital stimulation of another, and oral sex. While they are short of intercourse, these actions incite desire for sex and compromise areas God meant to be reserved for the marriage relationship alone.

Stick with us and we'll take a no-holds-barred look at this treacherous minefield a little later . . . if you have the courage.

Minefield 3: I Can Read or Watch Whatever I Want!

We live in a day when images we should avoid bombard us. Just think of what's out there for guys—*Sports Illustrated Swimsuit Edition,* MTV, *Playboy,* Internet porn, midriff-baring tops and jeans that look as though they could slide off any minute. Flip on the television and what do you find? Hilarious shows like *Friends* have you laughing at every turn, but the situations imply sex without commitment and mostly without marriage. Popular shows like *Las Vegas* sizzle with plenty of cleavage and thigh to go around. On television, anyplace is seen as a good place to get it on with whomever—whenever. And this attitude isn't just found in fictional characters. The goal of reality dating shows like *Blind Date* and *The Fifth Wheel* is less about helping people find a mate than hoping they will get carried away in the hot tub.

So what's the big deal? The One who left us His footprints told us our eyes are also the windows of our souls. When we fill them with garbage, it will only be a matter of time until the garbage comes out in our lives. The images that fill our heads impact our attitudes and then affect our actions.

Minefield 4: Truth Can Be Bent to Fit Any Situation

Facts seem to be at the whim of the user. If telling the truth works, great! If it causes discomfort, just bend it! In his research for *Right from Wrong,* Josh McDowell surveyed church kids between the ages of eleven and eighteen. He found in the three months before his survey:

- 66 percent had lied to a parent, teacher, or other adult.
- 59 percent had lied to their peers.

This minefield tempts us to misstep by using truth, and untruth, to build ourselves up, get us out of awkward circumstances, make us look better than somebody else, or get what we really want whether we deserve it or not.

But Christ never left footprints leading in that direction.

Minefield 5: There's No Connection between Attending Church on Sunday and How I Live Monday through Saturday

We have turned life into a *TIME* magazine lifestyle. We have our "sports section," our "entertainment section," our "education section," and our *God section*—each one independent of the other and standing on its own. God never meant for life to be compartmentalized. Everything we do influences every part of who we are.

Too often it's like that with our Christian life. When we go to church on Sunday morning, we act all the right ways and say all the right things. But we sound totally different in the locker room at school on Monday, or we act totally different on a Friday night date. Sitting in youth group on Sunday night we talk about the importance of honesty, but when we don't know the answers to our exam, we have no problem looking over at the paper of our friend sitting next to us. We bend the standards of truth to accomplish the goal: decent grades (we hope!).

Hope Amidst the Mines

Some of us are standing on the edge of the minefields ready to wander in. Others of us, like missionary Jim Humphries and the two soldiers, find ourselves already surrounded by minefields with no idea of how to get out.

Here's the good news! Jesus Christ knew we would end up there. That's why He left us His footprints and gave us His Word. So come on a journey with us and let's find out how to be a man of character who will impact our world. Let's look together at how God made each of us to be a world changer. As you walk with Him you will see things happen in your life only God could do!

I think you'll love the trip!

The Ultimate Prize

ANDY

In 1998 I had the privilege of being a part of what some people call the greatest team in baseball history. Our New York Yankees team won what was then an American League record: 114 games. Going into the postseason we knew none of that would matter if we didn't win the World Series. And winning the series was our only goal. When you play for the Yankees, any year you don't win the World Series is a failure, regardless of the regular season. Our journey toward the World Series started with a sweep of the Texas Rangers in the American League Division Series. We blew through the series, giving up a grand total of one run in the three games combined. Cleveland gave us a harder time in the American League Championship Series, but we still won in six games. This set up a showdown with the National League Champion San Diego Padres in the World Series.

We played the first two games in Yankee Stadium. David Wells was the starting and winning pitcher for Game 1. On days I don't start I sit with the rest of the team in the dugout. But not during the '98 series. I caught an emergency flight back home to Houston when my mom called me after Game 1 and told me my dad needed open-heart surgery. Suddenly baseball and the World Series didn't matter. My only concern was my father.

I stayed with my dad as long as I could, but I had to return to the team to pitch Game 4. My father was sick, but I still had to do my job. The Yankees won the first three games and needed only one more victory to clinch our second World Championship in three years. After flying from Houston to San Diego I tried to go through all my normal routine before a start. But, to be honest, I really wasn't thinking about baseball. All I could think about was my dad. As I walked out onto the pitcher's mound I dedicated the game to him. I don't know how I did it, but I didn't give up a single run through seven innings. Our manager, Joe Torre, brought in relievers Jeff Nelson and Mariano Rivera to pitch the final two innings. They shut down the Padres and we won the game 3–0, completing the World Series sweep.

The New York Yankees were world champions, and I was the winning pitcher of the deciding game; but none of that registered with me at the time. I felt numb. As soon as the game was over I went into the clubhouse and called my dad. He'd watched the game on television and we talked about how I'd done. He told me he was proud of me and then he told me he felt fine. Right then I knew he was going to be OK. For the first time in a long time I could finally relax. All the pressure lifted, the pressure of a 162-game season, the play-offs, and the series, but most important, the pressure of worrying about my dad. God took it all away and gave me peace.

Because my dad was doing much better I didn't have to rush to the airport to catch a plane back to Houston. My wife, Laura, and I decided to enjoy the moment and join the team for our victory celebration in a San Diego ballroom. The place was packed with people who were going around shaking hands and slapping each other on the back and celebrating our win. Laura and I relaxed at a table and took it all in. We wanted to savor the moment. Strangers constantly came up to our table to ask if they could have their picture taken with us. Most of the time we smiled and let them.

But then in the middle of the party, a woman I'd never met came up and asked Laura, "I'm sorry to bother you, but do you mind if I kiss your husband?" Laura didn't have to answer. I cut the woman off and said, "I don't think that would be appropriate." After she left Laura turned to me and asked, "If women act like this while I'm with you, what are they like when I'm not around?"

You can probably guess the answer. Women aren't shy about throwing themselves at professional athletes. That's how temptation is. You don't have to go looking for it. It will come looking for you. And it usually waits for moments like this. I was physically and emotionally drained after a grueling season and the agony of wondering if my father would survive his surgery. My thoughts weren't focused on God. They weren't focused anywhere. I was too tired to focus. But temptation didn't care. It waited until I was at my weakest and then it struck. You don't have to be a big league ballplayer for this to happen. None of us has to go out of our way to find a situation where we'll be tempted. Just wait. It'll find you.

That's why you and I have to always be on our guard. We can't wait until we're in the middle of some situation we can't handle to get serious about following Jesus. And that's what we are really talking about when we talk about purity. This is more than a question of saying no to sex until you are married or not drinking alcohol. It goes beyond resisting temptation or cleaning up your language. All that is secondary to something much bigger and more important. Living a life of purity means getting serious about God and living in a way that honors Jesus Christ.

How Serious Are You?

I didn't wait until I made it to the big leagues to commit myself to honoring Christ with my life. If I had waited until I made the Yankees in 1995, it would have been too late. No, this was a decision I made back in high school when I decided I was serious about being a Christian.

I grew up hearing about Jesus, but my family didn't go to a church that emphasized having a personal relationship with Him. That idea was completely new to us. My sister was the first person in our family to experience this kind of relationship. She went to a revival at a Baptist church in our town and came home talking about getting saved. I listened to what she said and decided to check it out for myself. Not long after, I asked Jesus to forgive me of my sin and to become my Lord and Savior. I was eleven at the time. Pretty soon my mom and dad started going to church with my sister and me, and they were saved as well.

Being a Christian is a cinch when you're eleven. But once I got into high school it wasn't so easy. The friends I'd grown up with and played baseball with every summer started doing things I knew I couldn't be a part of, not if I was serious about Jesus. In my junior and senior years of high school I had to make some decisions about who I would be. I had friends I'd known all my life and suddenly we were going in different directions. I had to decide whether I wanted to run with guys I knew would bring me down.

It wasn't easy separating myself from these guys who'd been my friends all through grade school and junior high, but I couldn't call myself a Christian and do what they were doing. I faced a tough choice. And it wasn't just a decision of which crowd I would run with. In that moment I had to choose what kind of relationship I wanted to have with God. Did I want Him to be someone I called out to when times were tough, only to ignore Him the rest of the time as I lived however I wanted? Or did I want to live my life for Him, to honor Him in everything I do? In the end there wasn't a choice. For me the bottom line is this: what's the point of getting saved and making a commitment to Christ if you aren't going to live the way God wants you to live? Why live a lie? If you're going to say you're a Christian, live it. Don't be a phony. Walk the walk.

That's what this entire book comes down to. We're just in the first chapter, but I might as well be straight with you. This whole question of purity isn't about how true love waits until you are married to have sex. You can do that and still miss the point. Purity begins with a commitment to live in a way that honors Jesus Christ, a commitment that spreads over every part of your life. A life of purity means honoring the Lord in the language you use, the movies you watch, the way you conduct yourself in class. It's a total package. The Bible says to do everything for the glory of God (1 Corinthians 10:31). That's what purity is all about. Unless you are willing to do that, you might as well stop reading right now.

I don't want to come across like some sort of supersaint. By myself I can't follow through on this commitment anymore than you can. But God doesn't leave us by ourselves. I found once I made up my mind to stay true to God no matter what anyone else did, God blessed my life. He made it where pressure from friends wasn't that hard for me to deal with. When you're in high school, it seems like you're constantly worrying about other people's opinions. But God took that fear away from me. He blessed me by making me strong enough to stand alone even at a young age.

Thankfully I wasn't really taking a stand by myself. My mom and dad and sister stood with me. We were all saved around the same time and went to church together as a family. Then, when I was fifteen, I started dating the girl who is now my wife. Her dad was my pastor, and I was very close to her three older brothers. I looked up to all of them and the walk they had with Christ. They inspired me to aim higher. I also knew even then that I wanted to marry Laura one day, and I didn't want to do anything to blow that. Just dating her and being around her family made the Lord even more important to me.

Our Most Precious Possession

But it wasn't just Laura or my family and friends that kept me close to God. As I grew in my relationship with Him I began to see the value of my testimony. Our testimonies are more than the story of how we were saved. A testimony is the outward evidence other people see in us of the faith we say we have in God. Our actions tell them everything they need to know about how real Jesus actually is. Only when our actions match our commitment will people listen to what we have to say about God. The

Lord started showing me how being in the wrong place, even if I wasn't doing what everyone else was doing, would make it impossible for me to tell other people about Him. It's a case of guilt by association. If I hung out with my friends who were drinking, everyone who saw me there would assume I was drinking too. They'd think I wasn't any different from anyone else. How could I ever tell any of them about how Jesus changed my life after that?

Living consistently for Christ didn't come easily in high school. It still doesn't. Satan wants nothing more than to make you and me look like phonies. Like I said, when you're a ballplayer you don't have to go looking for temptation, it comes looking for you. And it's not just in the majors. After high school I played one season of college ball before being drafted by New York. The Yankees immediately sent me to play for their rookie league team in Tampa, Florida. Playing baseball in the minor leagues is brutal. We had to make ten- and eleven-hour bus trips between cities when we went on the road. There was a lot of down time during the day before games, and afterwards guys on the team wanted to hit the bars.

This really put me in a hard spot. All of us want to be accepted, and in sports you have to be part of the team, especially in baseball. During the season I'm around my teammates more than I'm around anyone else. When we go on the road we're with one another 24/7. Being a part of the team doesn't just mean wearing the same uniform. You work together toward a common goal and build friendships with each other. And that's where honoring Christ with our lives gets tough. Sometimes we allow our desire to be accepted put us in the middle of places we don't need to be.

Yet I've found you don't have to go along with the crowd to be accepted by the team. Staying true to the Lord doesn't mean you have to become a thorn in everyone's side. On the team, I'm one of the guys. My teammates have a good time being around me, but they know where I stand. More importantly, they respect me for my faith because I strive to be consistent. I also work hard on the field and give the team everything I've got. All my talk of God doesn't mean a thing if I don't. Your life also has to match what you say on and off the field. If you aren't consistent, your words are nothing but noise.

Focusing on What Matters

A life of purity means a commitment to honor Christ with your life. You can count on this commitment being tested every single day. I had a couple of pretty good years in 1996 and 1997. In '96 I won more than twenty games for the first time and finished second for the American League Cy Young award. The next season I won eighteen games and my earned run average stayed in the mid-2 range. After these seasons, with all my success, I had the opportunity to start doing endorsements and making appearances. Companies would call and ask me to come and mingle with some of their clients at social functions. Accepting these offers would give me a chance to make more money and get my name out there. However, it would also mean sacrificing time I wanted to spend with my wife and family. So I passed. I couldn't let anything get in the way of what was most important to me.

If you really want to live a life that honors God, you have to keep your focus on what matters most to you. For me, my relationship with God and my relationship with my wife and family mean more to me than anything else. I can't let anything get in the way of either.

But that wasn't the only reason I turned down some of these opportunities. I knew if someone paid me to mingle at a company party it might put me in a bad situation. I didn't think I might fall to the temptation, but I knew just being there would damage my testimony. People think they know me because they've watched me play baseball on television, but they don't.

They don't know anything about me. If someone saw me at one of these parties, what was he going to think? He'd think I'm just like everyone else there, and my testimony would be shot. If God opened the door for me to witness to someone, I wouldn't be able to because he wouldn't think I had anything real to say.

The testimony we have for Jesus Christ is the most valuable gift we will ever be given. It's too valuable to throw away, or to compromise. And that's what a life of purity comes down to. That's why daily I ask for God's wisdom and strength in the decisions that I make and the things that I do. I want people to see Christ in me. It's a daily battle when you walk with the Lord, for me or for anyone, but it's worth the effort. I know you'll find it will be for you as well.

Study Questions

- Why does purity matter to you? What makes it important? Does your life show that it is?
- Where does temptation hit you with the greatest force? What areas of your purity are most vulnerable to attack? What would help you get out of the minefields these temptations thrust you into?
- How does your life Monday through Saturday compare to your church attendance on Sunday? Do your actions reflect the attitudes and priorities of a Christ-follower? Why or why not?
- Find 1 Corinthians 10:31 in your Bible and read it two or three times. Now read 1 Peter 1:13–16. What does it mean to be holy? What does holiness look like in the everyday life of a guy? How does living a holy life relate to "doing everything for the glory of God"? And just in case you didn't catch on, holiness and living for the glory of God are the heart of a life of purity. Does this describe your life? Would you like for it to? This isn't just about receiving Christ as your Savior.

We're asking you to commit yourself to live in a way that honors Jesus Christ in everything you do. Will you do this right now?

Living beyond the Moment

CHAPTER TWO

Are You Prepared for Life's Final Exam?

BOB

Why do we only learn some lessons the hard way?

I remember one hard lesson like it was yesterday. There I sat taking a final exam at the end of the first semester of my freshman year at Indiana University. And I didn't have a clue what the answers might be.

But, hey, did I really care? The last few months had been a blast, a fun entry into college. Classes and studying just sort of interrupted the good time I was having. Was I sowing wild oats or distracting myself from family pain? (At the end of that semester I received one of only two letters I ever got in my lifetime from my father . . . but that's another story.) Whatever! Anyway, here I sat after lots of fun but almost no time cracking the books.

As I stared at the first few questions on the final exam, sweat beaded across my forehead. My mouth became drier than the Mojave Desert. I reached up to loosen my collar but, yikes, it was already wide open. Then I felt my armpits getting moist, my breathing becoming shallow, and my vision blurring. And reality sunk in—I didn't know anything this test was asking!

As my life flashed before me, I knew I shouldn't have had such a good time that semester, especially the weekend before the final. I was light-headed with the realization that how I'd spent my time was going to be obvious to the professor when he graded this exam. It was in that sobering moment that I recognized the wisdom behind one of life's critical truths: *always begin with the end in mind!*

It's true about tests; it's true about life in general. And it's definitely true about our spiritual life.

Accountability Is Part of Life's Game

No matter where we are in our journey, accountability comes with the turf. For the student, it's finals, SATs, and graduation qualifications. For the college graduate, it's the outcome of job interviews. For the employee, it's the annual job performance review often based on sales reports, revenue, cost efficiencies, and so on. For the doctor, it's the success, or failure, of medical procedures. And for the lawyer, it's, "Did you win or lose the case?"

And it's not just in the marketplace! My friend, Andy, is one of the greatest pitchers in major league baseball. Yet in every game he's judged by strikeouts, base on balls, earned run averages, and innings pitched. The same thing holds true in other arenas . . .

- In football, it's yards gained, pass completion percentage, quarterback sacks, and third down conversions.
- In hockey, it's goals, checks, and hat tricks.
- In government, the scorecard of accountability is votes received, legislation introduced, legislation enacted, and, "Did I do a good enough job to get reelected?"

The bottom line is that *whatever* we do we always have to answer for how we did, what we did (or didn't do), and how we measure up. We're always held accountable. God makes it clear in His Word that all of us will ultimately answer to Him for how we played the game of life. Scripture teaches that every Christian will one day stand before the Lord and give an account at what Scripture calls *the judgment seat*. Listen to Romans 14:10 and 12, "For we will all stand before the judgment seat of God. . . . Each of us will give an account of himself to God." This will be our final exam with God. There will be no sliding into it like I did in my freshman final, no opportunity for second chances or cramming for the test. God's exam will take a long look at how each of us lived our lives. We won't be measured against one another. No, the standard God will use is the unchanging standard of His owner's manual for life, the Bible. Since this is true, we need to live with that end in mind.

You Better Know the Material Covered

One thing I figured out about tests in school is that it always helps to know what material will be covered on the exam. It didn't make any difference what I hoped would be covered or what I wished the teacher had asked. It was my responsibility to find out what material I would be tested on and then to learn it!

God makes it very clear in the Bible what material we need to know for His final exam. Listen to 1 Corinthians 3:11–15: "No one can lay any other foundation than what has been laid—that is, Jesus Christ. If anyone builds on the foundation with gold, silver, costly stones, wood, hay, or straw, each one's work will become obvious, for the day will disclose it, because it will be revealed by fire; the fire will test the quality of each one's work. If anyone's work that he has built survives, he will receive a reward. If anyone's work is burned up, it will be lost, but he will be saved; yet it will be like an escape through fire."

Paul compares your life and mine to the building of a structure. Every building must have a secure and solid foundation if it is to stand. Paul clearly states there is only ONE foundation upon which the Christian life can be built—the person and work of Jesus Christ.

Take a moment and notice an important point. The foundation for your life is not "Christ *plus* anything." Not "Christ *plus* baptism" or "Christ *plus* church attendance" or "Christ *plus* prayer, Bible study, and Scripture memorization." While all those things are important as you grow as a Christian, the *only* thing that makes you or me a Christian to begin with is simply inviting Christ into our lives as Savior and Lord!

Some of us are OK with the part about Christ as Savior, but the deal about Lord is a little too much too fast. They want to punch their card by recognizing Christ's desire for a relationship with them; they just don't want Him infringing on any and every area of life. To acknowledge Him on Sunday, that's OK; but on dates . . . you've got to be kidding! To have somebody say a prayer at meals, no problem. But to invite Christ along when it's just the guys . . . *c'mon!*

But Jesus says He wants to be Savior *and* Lord. Not just one without the other. It's a package deal. *He's either Lord of all . . . or not at all.* He doesn't respond well to our putting NO TRESPASSING signs on areas of our lives. He expects access to it all. When Paul challenges Christ-followers to present their bodies as living sacrifices to Christ in Romans 12:1–2, he's referring to the burnt offering in the Old Testament. It's the one offering in which the *entire* animal was burned up on the altar. Every part of it. In the same way, Paul says every area of our lives is to be Christ's.

If you're wondering how you can know if Jesus is Lord of all in your life, here's a simple test. Can you say with the apostle Paul that you aren't "trying to please men but God, who tests our hearts" (1 Thessalonians 2:4 NIV)? Here's another key: Have you made the goal of your life to please Him (2 Corinthians 5:9)? When that's the case, you'll have no problem with lordship.

But that is just the beginning. From the moment we receive Christ through the rest of our lives, you and I are constructing a building. No building is better than the materials used to construct it. The passage above tells us we all will use one of two different types of materials. We will either build our lives out of wood, hay, or straw—inferior materials which won't last—or we will build them out of high quality and valued materials—gold, silver, or jewels.

How can we build our lives out of gold and silver rather than dried up old straw? God will judge the quality of the materials with which we build our lives in three areas:

1. Our Motivations

It's not just what we do, but *why* we do what we do that's important. In 1 Corinthians 4:5 Paul tells us when the Lord comes, He will "both bring to light what is hidden in darkness and reveal the intentions of the hearts. And then praise will come to each one from God." Just going through the motions of doing what's right or what people expect from us doesn't cut it!

2. Our Actions

We will all answer deed by deed for everything we've done in our lives. In 2 Corinthians 5:10 Paul reminds us, "For we must all appear before the judgment seat of Christ, so that each may be repaid for what he has done in the body, whether good or bad." Our actions do count. God holds us responsible for everything we do, even the things we say. Matthew 12:36 tells us we will give an account for every idle word we have spoken in our lives. This doesn't mean God lets us into heaven based on what we've done for Him. Jesus did everything that needs to be done for us to be saved when He died on a cross for our sins. As believers, we will either be rewarded for what we do for Christ, or we will be left standing before Him empty-handed. And what will we do with those rewards? The last book of the Bible tells us we will throw our rewards at the feet of Jesus as a way of worshipping Him. I don't know about you, but I don't want to be found empty-handed.

3. Our Contributions

God has given every believer at least one spiritual gift, that is, a special ability with which we can serve God and other people. You may not yet know what your gift is, but you have at least one and you will discover it (or them) someday soon. God expects us to use the gifts He gives, and we will answer for how we use God's gift in service to others. After all, Christ clearly taught that the way to be great in the kingdom of God is to be a servant to others (Matthew 23:11–12; Mark 10:43–44). He holds us accountable for how well we follow His example.

When we answer to God, Christ Himself will give us the final exam. The passage in 1 Corinthians we looked at a moment ago tells us our works will be tested by fire. Throughout Scripture fire is the testing agent of God to see whether something is pure and authentic. The fire which will test the quality of our works comes from Jesus Himself. We see the source of that fire in Revelation chapter 1 when the apostle John sees the vision of the risen Christ. As he stands before Christ, John describes Jesus' eyes as "a blazing fire" (Revelation 1:14 NIV). Even before we ultimately stand before Christ for our final exam, God's eyes examine our hearts. In the Old Testament we are told, "For the eyes of the LORD range throughout the earth to show Himself strong for those whose hearts are *completely* His" (2 Chronicles 16:9, *italics mine*).

So even while we're living, Christ is concerned about *what* we do, but even more so about *why* we do it!

Life's Final Exam

The fact that we answer to Jesus Christ Himself for what we do is stunning and sobering. This is our accountability above all other accountabilities. No matter who our actions may hurt or let down, when we ignore God's guidelines for life we ultimately break the heart of God. This truth helps explain a couple of interesting twists in Scripture.

In the book of Genesis a man named Joseph followed God and tried to please Him no matter how his life went. His brothers hated him and sold him as a slave. Eventually Joseph ended up working for a man named Potiphar. Yet Joseph kept following God, and his boss noticed. Potiphar knew he could trust Joseph completely, and he had Joseph work in his home unsupervised. But Joseph was also a good-looking guy. It didn't take long for Potiphar's wife to notice. One day when no one else was around, she grabbed Joseph and begged him to go to bed with her. Listen to Joseph's answer: "No one in this house is greater than I am. He has withheld nothing from me except you, because you are his wife. So how could I do such a great evil and *sin against God?*" (Genesis 39:9, *italics mine*).

If Joseph had to explain why he wouldn't have sex with his boss's wife, why didn't he just say that he would be betraying his boss? Wouldn't that be convincing enough to explain his rejection of her? No, Joseph knew that his ultimate accountability was to God who had put him in this position to begin with. There would be no higher source of accountability than to stand before God and to give an answer for not only the *what* but the *why* of his life's choices.

Another man in the Old Testament was tempted to sleep with another man's wife, but, unlike Joseph, he gave in to temptation. King David was walking on the roof of his palace one night and noticed a woman named Bathsheba. He sent his men who brought her back to his room. A few weeks later she sent word to David telling him she was pregnant. To make matters worse, she was married to one of David's soldiers who was off fighting a war at the time. David hid his sin for a year, even sending Bathsheba's husband to the front lines where he was killed.

When he was confronted by Nathan the prophet, David finally broke down and confessed the wrong he'd done by having sex with another man's wife and then ordering her husband's murder to try to cover it up. He realized he'd sinned against Bathsheba herself by seducing her and getting her pregnant. He even realized he'd sinned against Israel by betraying the confidence of the people who trusted him as their king. But even higher than that he was ultimately responsible to the Giver of life and the Judge of everything we do. He understood that he would ultimately give an account to Almighty God for the actions of his life—*just like you and me.*

As David pours out his confession in Psalm 51, he begs God to forgive him of where he has stepped over the line of God's guidelines for effective living. He reaches the height of his agony, "Against You—You alone—I have sinned and done this evil in Your sight" (Psalm 51:4).

So How Are You Preparing for Life's Final Exam?

Have you read some new ideas in this chapter? Maybe you already knew them, but you just weren't applying them to your life. Or maybe you've got some unsettled feelings in your gut. You're nervous about facing God—wondering if you'll be ready for that final exam of your life. To say you'd be embarrassed is the understatement of the decade. Answering to Jesus Christ? Making your life's goal to please God? Explaining why you did or didn't conduct your life that way? It will be a sobering encounter—a much bigger deal than the day I tried to fake my way through a final that I wasn't the least bit ready to take! I hope you'll be better prepared than I was for the test at Indiana University.

Oh, by the way, I learned it's way too late to get ready for an exam on the day you have to take it!

Seize Tomorrow

ANDY

The off-season for major league baseball players is officially four and a half months. Not mine. My last off-season lasted all of two weeks. Sometimes I'll take as many as three weeks after the season ends to just lay around and take it easy. But by the end of November or the first of December it's time to get back in the gym and start getting ready for the next season. It may seem a little crazy to start working out around Thanksgiving when the first game of the season isn't until April, but I'm not trying to get ready for games in April or May. I work out in November for games in October. I don't want to start off sharp and fade as the season wears on. My goal is to peak when games mean the most and, hopefully, help my team win the World Series.

Staying strong throughout a long season can be a challenge. God blessed me by allowing me to start my major league career with the New York Yankees at the beginning of a fantastic run. We made the play-offs at the end of my rookie year in 1995, but that was only the beginning. Between 1996 and 2003 we played in six World Series, winning four. During my nine seasons with the Yankees I made thirty career postseason starts. Keep in mind most pitchers only make around thirty starts in a season, which means I have an extra season of wear on my body. All those additional games take their toll, which is probably why I've battled injuries at different times during my career.

My off-season workouts changed when Roger Clemens joined the Yankees in 1998. Roger showed me how a strenuous workout routine not only produces more wins during the season; it can also prolong a career. That's when I started working out with him. Roger and I don't just go out in the yard and play catch. We start our two-hour sessions by working hard on cardiovascular exercises. That usually means running two or three miles. Then Brian, our strength and conditioning coach, will have us work on different parts of our body. One day we lift weights with our legs. Another day we work on the upper body along with some agility work. And we do ab work—a *lot* of ab work. Brian has us do power sit-ups and crunches and other exercises that work muscles most people don't even know they have. Yet each of these muscles is important because of the torque throwing a baseball puts on the body. In fact, my fastball jumped three miles an hour to around ninety-three or ninety-four as a result of these exercises. After Roger and I both signed with the Houston Astros before the 2004 season, we added batting practice to our daily routine along with additional cardio work.

I have to be honest. Some mornings I would rather stay in bed or lay around the house because I know it's the *off*-season. Without a game on the schedule there's not a lot of urgency to motivate me to get out and run a couple of miles. And then I think about how years ago pitchers never lifted weights or even picked up a baseball from the moment the season ended until Spring Training started in February. There are times I wonder why I don't just sit on the couch and eat all day instead of working so hard.

So why do I push myself when I could be relaxing? I do it because I'm not just thinking about what I want to do today or tomorrow. No, I'm thinking about what I want to accomplish next season and through the rest of my career. When you focus only on today you make poor decisions and end up mortgaging tomorrow. To be successful in life, especially in your Christian life, you have to think long term. You have to keep your sights on your ultimate goals and plot a course to reach them.

Living for God's Ultimate Purpose

My ultimate goal as a ballplayer is to win the World Series. Period. When I played for the Yankees we didn't just hope to make it to the series at the end of the season. We *expected* to play in it and win it every season. Nothing changed when I left New York. I signed with the Astros after the 2003 season because I wanted to help bring a championship to my hometown. That's why I play the game.

As a Christian I also have one goal. I want to fulfill God's purpose for my life. I constantly ask myself "What does God want me to do?" and "Where does He want me to go?" Those may sound like odd questions to ask in a book about purity. After all, doesn't purity just mean sexual purity? Hardly. As I said in the last chapter, living a pure life means trying to please God in everything I do. And the best way to please God is living in a way He can work through me and use me in other people's lives.

The question of God's purpose for my life both today and for the rest of my life makes everything else secondary, even baseball. Don't get me wrong. I know the Lord wants me to play baseball. After all, a man needs to have a job. But my career won't last forever. Eventually my life will take another turn. When that time comes, God's plan for me and my family will come first. With every decision I make I have to think about what the long-term effects will be. Being able to discern this requires a pure and holy heart before God.

While God has me playing baseball, even where I play comes down to a question of His plan for my life. When my last contract with the Yankees expired I could sign with any major league team I wanted. But I knew that wasn't really my decision. I prayed and sought God's will throughout the 2003 baseball season because I wanted to know where God wanted me to play next. Honestly, I could never imagine playing anywhere but New York. But God could. He wanted me in Houston. I thought I knew why when I signed, but I only saw the tip of the iceberg. One month before the start of Spring Training, one of my best friends found out he had cancer. The Lord planted me in Houston to be there for him and his family.

I didn't know life would take this kind of turn when I was trying to decide whether to play for the Yankees or the Astros. God did. That's why living for God's long-term purposes and plan for your life is so important. And you can't do that without striving to have a pure heart before Him.

Thinking beyond the Moment

Living for tomorrow isn't easy, especially when it comes to the one area of your life where your commitment to purity will face its greatest test: sex. I know thinking about tomorrow feels crazy when your hormones kick in and you really want to give in to temptation. Yet in that moment is when you have to think long term. The decisions you make today put into motion a chain of consequences, some of which you will live with the rest of your life. The thing you want so badly today that it consumes all of your thoughts may well be the choice you regret forever. That's why you have to think beyond the moment. Purity demands you think in terms of a lifetime.

I know this sounds pretty old-fashioned. After all, a lot of guys think if they are careful and their girlfriends don't get pregnant they've escaped any negative consequences. They are wrong. We live in a world that makes sex outside of marriage sound like the greatest thing ever. In the eyes of many, pro athletes live a fantasy life where they can have any woman they want. You may have heard some ballplayers talk about how they can walk into a bar and choose a girl like walking through a buffet line. One night they sleep with a blonde, the next a redhead. All they have to do is pick one out. Guys talk about this lifestyle like it is a dream come true.

I once had a teammate who jumped into the sex and party life with nothing held back. He would brag in the clubhouse about how he would never get married and be tied down to only one woman. But then, when the two of us were alone, he would tell me, "Andy, honestly man, I wish I had what you have." He knew the fun of a promiscuous lifestyle is really an illusion. It can't satisfy anyone. It leaves emptiness. That's how every sin is. Satan tries to make us believe he can give us everything we could ever want. But he is a liar. He can't give us anything but death.

You might be thinking this doesn't really apply to you because you don't plan to start sleeping around. Instead you just want to give into temptation this one time with a girl you think might be the one. Besides, God promises to forgive us when we confess our sin to Him. Doesn't that mean He will forgive you of this sin as well? Of course He will. I believe once you become a Christian nothing can take away your salvation. But if you use His promise to forgive as an excuse to do whatever you want, you've missed the whole point of the life Jesus died to give you. Like I said before, if you claim to be a Christian, live it! God isn't in to making you feel good all the time and letting you do whatever you want. His plan is for you and me to be more and more like Jesus. You and I will stand before God one day to answer for everything we've ever done. I know I'm going to be ashamed of a lot of stuff I've done already. Why would I want to keep adding on to the pile?

Every sin has consequences, and those consequences don't always go away when God forgives us. If you kill someone you have to go to prison. But if you get saved that doesn't mean you get out of prison. Galatians 6:7–8 says, "Don't be deceived: God is not mocked. For whatever a man sows he will also reap, because the one who sows to his flesh will reap corruption from the flesh, but the one who sows to the Spirit will reap eternal life from the Spirit." When it comes to sexual sin, these consequences go beyond surprise pregnancies and diseases, especially for a believer.

Right now your mind might lock onto how great it would be to have sex, but ultimately you're going to want much more in your relationship with your future wife. Good marriages are built on trust and respect. If you can't control yourself now, before you get married, how can your future spouse trust you later on? I think about this with Laura. She never worries about what might happen to me during road trips because she trusts me completely, and I would never do anything to violate that trust. That might not sound like a big deal to you now, but believe me, it will someday. And then there's the whole issue of respect. You completely lose this when you can't control yourself before you get married.

When you call yourself a Christian you want even more out of marriage. Ultimately you want God's blessing on your life. I don't believe that a lot of people who have lived together or had sex before they got married have the kind of marriage that God would want them to have. I don't think His blessing is on that kind of marriage. God is forgiving, and if you've had premarital sex God will forgive you. I don't think He will take away all His blessings from your marriage or torture you in your marriage. But, you've still sinned and it's not what God wants us to do. You're starting out on the wrong foot completely. Moreover, you may have to reap what you've sown one way or another in your life. It may not happen that exact day, but it could happen in the future.

This Isn't about You

The choices you make don't affect you alone. Your life is interconnected with people, some of whom you don't even know yet. Living for tomorrow means thinking about the impact your choices will have on their lives. This was something I constantly thought about when Laura and I were dating. She wasn't just my girlfriend. Her dad was my pastor then and he still is today. I've always looked up to him as one of the godliest men I've ever met. Growing up under his preaching I learned many, many things about God. As a high school kid who loved the Lord, I held him up to a very high standard. My respect for him as my pastor and my girlfriend's father kept me from trying things I knew could destroy his ministry. I didn't want to do anything to bring shame on him or his ministry or his family.

Even if you don't date your pastor's daughter you should think about how your actions with your girlfriend will affect her family. You need to think also about how the things you do on your dates could impact her future spouse, and yours. Some guys justify going further physically with a girl than they know God would want them to by saying they are in love and will probably get married. Listen, even if you are engaged, you do not have any right to your girlfriend's body. First Corinthians 7:4 says, "A wife does not have authority over her own body, but her husband does. Equally, a husband does not have authority over his own body, but his wife does." Until you say, "I do," you don't really know she is the one. You can't take things that don't belong to you. You have no right to her body and she doesn't to yours because you aren't yet married.

Your choices will also affect the lives of your future children. You may try to convince your girlfriend that taking your relationship to the next level is no big deal, but I can guarantee you won't feel that way when you have a daughter of your own. Someday your kids will come to you and they'll ask about the kinds of things you did when you were dating. I want to set an example for my kids. I want them to be able to look up to me as a man of integrity. But all of that could come crumbling down if I couldn't look them in the eye when they start asking about how I acted as a teenager.

Touching Other Lives

Living for tomorrow also makes me look beyond myself to the people God wants to touch through my life. In the last chapter I talked about the power of your testimony. It is the most valuable thing you will ever have, although a lot of guys never give it a thought. You need to. I always want to be in a place where He can use me to talk to other people about Him. I'm not one of those guys who gets real loud and smashes guys in the head with God. Sometimes I wish I was a little more outspoken, but I'm not. I probably never will be. Instead I try to live for Christ as openly as I can. Then, as He gives me opportunities, I speak up.

Sometimes people who know me pretty well will come up to me privately and talk about stuff going on in their lives. They'll ask me to pray for them when they're facing surgery or when someone in their family is sick. I've had guys come to me who I never thought would want to talk about God, but they start searching for answers when they are hurting. No one looks for God when they are on the mountaintop, but everyone searches for Him when they go through a valley. Other times they just want to talk about the directions their lives are headed. They come to me because they know me and how I live my life. I've earned their respect, and they know I won't take a judgmental stance.

That's why I watch my life. Sure, I do the basics like not using profanity or hanging out in bars. It's not just that I would have to answer to God for those someday. I know if I did those things it would completely blow any chance I have of being used by God right now. But avoiding bad stuff is not enough. I want my teammates to see Jesus in me through the decisions I make and the priorities in my life. The Christian life isn't just a bunch of "don'ts." Purity is so much more. And that's what I try to show the people around me. I want people to see Christ's character in me. Only then will anyone listen when I try to tell them about God. They won't listen if they think I'm just like everyone else. I don't want to blow someone's chance of hearing about Jesus Christ. Some of our choices today can affect their eternities.

Keeping the long view in mind will change every part of your life. It changes the way you treat everything that is important to you. It changes the way you plan your future and decide what kind of career you want to have. It changes the way you look at sex. It changes the way you look at your entire life. Like I said, you have to continually ask God what He wants you to do and where He wants you to be. You can't just live for the moment and throw away your future. With every decision you have to carefully focus on God's plan for your life, then you set your sights on getting there.

Study Questions

- Read 1 Corinthians 3:10–17. The building in this passage refers to your life and what you do with it. What is the difference between a building constructed of gold, silver, and precious stones and one made of wood, hay, or straw? Look at your own life. What kind of building are you working on? What kinds of materials are you using? Examine not only what you do and why you do it. Also think about the gifts and abilities God has given you. What are you doing with them? Will the things to which you are devoting your life last beyond right now? How does the building of your life look to God?
- What is your ultimate goal as a follower of Jesus Christ? Be honest with yourself and God. Don't give Andy's answer, give your own. What do you want to accomplish for God with this life He has given you?
- Reaching long-term goals requires discipline and hard work, the same kind of work Andy puts in toward becoming the best pitcher he can possibly be. How are you training for a lifetime of honoring God? What specific steps are you taking now, or you need to begin taking, to build up your spiritual

muscles? What will you have to say no to today to reach your long-term goals?

- Chapter 2 discussed how your life is interconnected with the lives of people around you. This means your actions don't just affect you. They have an impact on many others as well. What kind of impact is your life having on the lives of people around you? Bob also reminded us that God isn't just concerned about what we do. He cares even more about why we do it. How are your actions and attitudes influencing people around you? Think about the girls you date, your siblings, and your parents. What kind of impact are you making on their lives? Is this the impact you want to make? Why or why not? If not, what can you do to change this?

Attention
to Detail

CHAPTER THREE

What's the Big Deal
about Purity, Anyway?

BOB

At 2:09 p.m. on July 19, 1989, United Airlines flight 232 took off from Denver, Colorado. The day was beautifully clear as the DC-10 climbed and leveled off at a cruising altitude of 37,000 feet. The 295 passengers on board settled in for the flight to Chicago, and its ultimate destination, Philadelphia. Nothing about the flight suggested this was anything other than a routine trip, just another day in the life of air traffic in America.

That was until one hour and seven minutes into the flight. Suddenly a huge explosive noise caused the plane to shudder in midair. The number two engine, mounted on the plane's tail, inexplicably failed. Worse yet, the main hydraulic system ceased to function. But even that should have been no problem for a DC-10. The amazing plane has three independent hydraulic systems providing what pilots call "redundancies"—repetitive systems that back up one another. Theoretically, the main hydraulic system could go down and the plane should still be able to continue to fly because the three redundant systems are completely self-sufficient.

There was only one small problem: The explosion took out all three redundant hydraulic systems. The three converged in a four-foot square section near the tail in the back of the plane. The odds of anything going wrong within that small area were about *one billion to one.* But on July 19, 1989, the odds didn't mean a thing and the unthinkable happened.

Captain Al Haynes and the crew of United 232 lost complete control. The DC-10 wouldn't turn, slow down, bank to the right or left, or pitch up or down. If they ever did get on the ground the steering wouldn't work and the brakes wouldn't stop the hurtling aircraft.

Somehow the captain and crew did the impossible. By alternating the amount of thrust applied to the two remaining engines, Captain Haynes was able to regain enough control to fly the plane to Sioux City, Iowa. This left the crew with one more problem. The Sioux City airport didn't have a runway long enough for a DC-10. In spite of the odds, Captain Haynes brought the plane down on the longest runway available. Unfortunately, one wingtip touched the ground before the landing gear, throwing the plane into a fiery, cartwheeling crash. Even with the crash, 185 lives were saved, including the entire flight crew. Tragically, 110 people died.

Research would show that a fan disk in a number two engine had blown apart, breaking through the tail section of the plane and cutting all three hydraulic systems. Investigators traced the part back to a six-thousand-pound block of titanium used to produce the high-precision fan disks by the Aluminum Company of America. The meticulous tracking used in the production of aircraft parts was able to go all the way back to the specific fan disk made. Researchers found that a small amount of nitrogen had not completely dissolved in the molten titanium. The result: a microscopic vacuum that, with time and the stress of hundreds of landings and take-offs, failed and exploded tragically.

The fan disk had been flawless *except* for the one nitrogen bubble that, after seventeen years, destroyed a plane. Amazing, isn't it? One microscopic impurity was able to bring down a loaded plane filled with passengers all of whom were completely unaware of the danger posed by one tiny bubble.

So Who Cares about Impurity?

Webster's dictionary defines the word *pure* as "unmixed with any other matter; free from dust and dirt; blotless, stainless." It goes on to say that the very essence of being pure means the subject at hand contains nothing that doesn't belong. Something that is pure is completely free of anything that would weaken or pollute it. By its very definition, the word *pure* indicates someone is free from moral fault or guilt.

So what's the big deal about purity? It means a lot if you're depending on the purity and integrity of the parts of the plane in which you're flying to keep it in the air in one piece and deliver you safe and sound to your destination. And when you pick up a prescription from the pharmacy, you take it for granted that the pharmacist didn't mix in any extra ingredients, or give you the wrong pills. You want the right medicine and you want it unmixed, untainted, and unpolluted.

That's exactly what God wants from your character. Solid and reliable. Untainted. Sturdy and secure. He wants it unmixed, not stained by elements that are improper to the way He desires you to live, and free from fault.

That's what Jesus meant in the greatest sermon ever preached, the Sermon on the Mount. He said, "Blessed are the pure in heart, because they will see God" (Matthew 5:8). Jesus was saying that only those who have an unmixed, clear, and clean heart would see God in a personal way. The word *heart* doesn't refer to the muscle that pumps blood around your body. Jesus is talking about the center of your being which includes your mind, attitudes, actions, and motivations. Only the pure in heart can have a personal and intimate relationship with Him. That kind of relationship can never be won through going to church or carrying a Bible or praying out loud or doing any other religious activity. In fact, Jesus, in referring to the pure in heart, uses the word in the original language that says, "they alone" will have an intimate and growing relationship with Christ.

But how do we do that?

God's Standard or Ours?

For centuries there's been a wide divergence between God's standard for how to experience a personal relationship with Him and how some people have claimed it occurs. Far too many have believed they could fake their way to an eternal intimacy with God. The view has been that surely God would set the standard on a curve like the grading curve at school. And surely it would be bell shaped so that there would be a large average range. If we hit somewhere within that area of conduct and attitude—and we aren't much worse than the next guy—then we would slip in *OK* with a passing grade from God. We try to rationalize that if we simply do our best what more could God want?

The emphasis on such a view is that it all depends on what *we do*. It's all about us and what we DO . . . and not about Him and what He's already DONE. The difference of two little letters—*N* and *E*—change the whole focus.

God has never been impressed by what we do. While we spend our time trying to change our lives from the outside in, God is begging us to let Him change us from the inside out. While everybody around us looks on the outward appearance and what they see, God chooses to look deep down into the heart.

In the Old Testament, when God sent Samuel to choose a new king for Israel, Samuel looked at all of Jesse's sons and saw how handsome, athletic, and skilled they were (the outside perspective). Samuel just knew one of them must be God's choice for a new king. But God had a different plan in mind. He made it very clear to Samuel that while men are tempted to look on the external appearance of what looks good, smells good, makes common sense, and so forth, God looks on the internal aspects of the heart to find those whose hearts are right for Him to use.

This is from 1 Chronicles 28:9: "The LORD searches every heart and understands the intention of every thought. If you seek Him, He will be found by you, but if you forsake Him, He will reject you forever."

Or listen to 2 Chronicles 16:9 where God declares, "For the eyes of the LORD range throughout the earth to show Himself strong for those whose hearts are completely His." God is on the lookout for men whose hearts want to be pure before God and to be loyal to His plan for our lives.

The challenge is that we're trying to do it by our own methods and standards. But God has made it very clear throughout Scripture that if we try to do it from an external process of simply "doing the right things," we're in for a pretty high standard. In Matthew 5:48 God gives the standard of being acceptable by our actions and attitudes. Here it is: *"Be perfect, therefore, as your heavenly Father is perfect."*

So how do you measure up? Do you feel pretty confident and comfortable? If you want a pure life from the outside in, all you have to do is be perfect because that's the standard of a righteous, holy, and pure God. And if you think you can do that on your own, then I wish you good luck. But I've never found one person in life who could ever reach that standard.

Instead, God says, "I want to change you from the inside out." In case you're thinking, *That only happens to adults,* get real!

Let me shoot straight and be honest. I grew up being dragged to church every time the doors were open. Sometimes I felt like I needed a bed there. I learned the Bible stories and how Jesus died for my sins, rose from the dead, and wanted to come into my life. I had a pretty good handle on the data. And then at ten years of age my best friend made a public decision and said he had accepted Christ into his heart.

I watched everyone pat him on the back as he walked forward. It was pretty neat. And I decided I wanted to get in on that. I wasn't trying to deceive anybody; I just wanted to be a part of what everybody thought we should be doing. When I was asked about my "decision," I gave all the right answers. After all, I had mastered the stories. And then I set out to try to DO the right things as I moved into my teen years.

There was only one problem: a bunch of my friends were walking on the edge. The more I tried to do the right things, especially when people like my parents were watching, the less ability I found to do them. What I knew I should do I found I didn't want to do, or have the power internally to do. And what I knew that I shouldn't do, I found I wanted to do. Go figure!

So what did I do? I kept playing the game, going through the religious motions. I did what I knew people around church wanted me to do (at least while they were watching). I became a great play-actor.

Then I left for college. Nobody watched all the time. No one knew whether I went to church. While home had been pretty strict with the rules, there wasn't anybody to answer to at the state university. So I put on the mask when I needed it and left it off when I didn't. As the crowd and their influence grew, my ability to do what I had been taught shriveled. But the game played on and I became a pro at it. I was religious when I needed to be, and did whatever I wanted when I wasn't under observation.

There was only one problem. The more I played the game the more I discovered that I had no power internally to change when I wanted. The only thing I could sometimes make work was doing the "right" things externally for short periods. But the problem remained. I was unable to really change my heart. And the further I went the less I liked what I saw inside myself. My friends told me I was having a great time at the parties, running with the crowd, but truthfully, inside, I found myself anything but happy. The more I attempted *doing* the right things from the outside in, the more frustrated I became from the inside out.

It took some time, and a lot of tough experiences, but God brought me to the end of my rope. Finally I came to the admission that I was a fake. I realized I knew *about* Christ, but I had never really come to *know* Him. I had been depending on what I could *do* rather than on what Christ had *done* to give me a new beginning.

When I accepted Jesus into my life, the "want to" of my heart radically changed.

Getting the Heart Right so the Actions can Follow

When Jesus talked about having a pure heart, He referred to the innermost part of a man's life. He referred to a man's will and his thoughts, for that's what drives emotions. That's why in Proverbs 23:7, God says "as [a man] thinks within himself, so he is." It's the mind that sets in motion the emotions that will soon follow. So there has to be a change in the innermost part of a guy for his actions and attitudes to be pure before God.

The Bible clearly says that we're dealing with a loaded bomb when we're trying to work things out on our own from the outside in. Jeremiah said it well when he laid out the truth, "The heart is more deceitful than anything else and desperately sick—who can understand it?" (Jeremiah 17:9).

The problem is that we have an internal disease called sin. And like the bubble in the aircraft engine fan blade, even the smallest sin ruins the entire heart. Now we don't like to talk much about sin in the twenty-first century. We like to shove it into a closet or hide it under a rug and pretend it doesn't exist. It sounds so archaic and old-fashioned. But it's real. Sin is basically a self-centered nature that wants what we want, when we want it, and how we want it—regardless of what anybody (including God) has to say. We're born with this disease. No one has to teach us to be self-centered. Just watch a four-year-old when another four-year-old tries to take his toy. The sin comes out naturally.

The Minnesota Crime Commission—a purely secular organization—discovered exactly the same truth. In doing a major study on why crime continues to increase in the United States, part of their findings sound eerily close to what the Bible has to say! They reported: "Every baby starts life as a little savage. He is completely selfish and self-centered. He wants what he wants when he wants it. . . . deny these and he seethes with rage and aggressiveness, which would be murderous were he not so helpless. He is, in fact, dirty. He has no morals, no knowledge, no skills. *This means that all children, not just certain children are born delinquent.*"[3]

Even the experts agree we've got an internal problem. And the only way that problem can be changed is by God changing our hearts. That's why Paul said, "Therefore if anyone is in Christ, there is a new creation; old things have passed away, and look, new things have come" (2 Corinthians 5:17). That radical change occurs *only* when we admit to God we can't change our hearts ourselves, and trust in God alone to do what we could never do. Just trying to do better or resolving not to make the same mistakes next time will never be enough. You have to be changed from the inside out.

So let me ask you a question: Has your heart been changed by God? Or, are you still struggling with the same old stuff that all the other guys are struggling with?

- Do you sense that you have no ability to stand on your own two feet and go against the flow of popular opinion?
- Do you constantly make resolutions to change, but they always fall flat?
- Does the pressure of all the guys just seem too great to resist? Do you find yourself doing the same things as everyone else and having the same attitudes, even though you know they are wrong?
- Do you find yourself saying all the right, churchy-sounding words but you don't really buy into them? Do you find it impossible to live what you know to be the right attitudes and actions?
- Do you find yourself becoming more and more irritated with people—maybe even your parents—whose standards of right and wrong seem too restrictive to you?

If your answer to these is yes, you've got a heart problem. And you need a heart transplant. You need to exchange a dirty heart for a pure one. And the only surgeon who can do that is Jesus Christ.

If you aren't sure whether that radical change has ever taken place in your heart, I want to challenge you today to seriously consider praying something like this to God:

Lord Jesus, I need You. I admit that I am unable to be perfect, which I know is Your standard. I have to admit that there is sin in my life (things that I do, think, say, or know I should do and don't) that breaks Your heart. And I understand that the Bible teaches me that that sin has separated me from You.

I ask You to come into my life and give me a spiritual heart transplant. I want You to change me from the inside out. I admit I can't do this on my own. I need You, Almighty God, to carry out the change.

I want You to remove my dirty heart spiritually and exchange it for a clean and pure heart that will honor and

*obey You. I pray the same prayer that King David prayed,
"God, create a clean heart for me, and renew a steadfast
spirit within me" (Psalm 51:10).*
  Thank You, Lord Jesus.

Sweat the Small Stuff

ANDY

The difference between success and failure in the big leagues doesn't necessarily come down to talent or ability. I know there are a lot of pitchers out there who have more natural ability than I do. That's why early on in my career I started working as hard as I could to squeeze as much out of my body as possible. That's why I also pay attention to every little detail. In pitching, the slightest flaw makes the difference between a ground ball that will end an inning and a home run. I have to make sure I take the ball out of my glove in just the right way or my delivery will be thrown off. My front foot has to land before I release the ball so that I can create a certain amount of leverage and a downward plane to home plate. Even the way I grip the ball matters. If I squeeze too tight, the flight of the ball to the batter changes, and his ability to hit it.

The slightest variation in the smallest details can cause big problems. I had a bad outing one night in Anaheim because I could never get comfortable on the mound. Every pitcher's mound is different in every stadium. That night in Anaheim my front foot never hit the ground right, and I couldn't create any leverage or velocity. As a result I couldn't throw the ball where I wanted and every pitch came out high. I'm a ground-ball pitcher who doesn't give up many home runs, but I gave up two in that game, all because of how my front foot landed during delivery.

The Small Stuff Matters to God

Little things matter in pitching, and they matter in your walk with God. Success or failure in your commitment to Him to live a pure and holy life often comes down to how you do with the little things. You have to sweat the small stuff. Jesus Himself said, "I tell you that on the day of judgment people will have to account for every careless word they speak" (Matthew 12:36). That means God takes note of the smallest details of our lives, and we will answer to Him for them someday.

God isn't harsh. He pays attention to the little details of our lives because they show who we really are on the inside. Jesus once told His disciples, "The mouth speaks from the overflow of the heart. A good man produces good things from his storeroom of good, and an evil man produces evil things from his storeroom of evil" (Matthew 12:34–35).

Purity has to be more than an act. It has to be who we are on the inside because that's what really matters. The person we are on the inside is who we have to live with every day. And that's where the decision for purity has to be made: inside. I can go and play the game and look good on the outside because I surround myself with good people. But if it isn't true on the inside it won't matter, and I'll know it. The bottom line is this, you will never be happy if you aren't happy with yourself. And you will never be happy if you are one thing on the outside but someone else on the inside.

My parents gave me a huge advantage in this area. I grew up watching my mom and dad take care of the little things in their own lives. I grew up in an ideal situation. My mom and dad both set great examples for me even before they had a personal relationship with Christ. I never heard either of them cuss and I never saw them drink. They also taught me about a walk with Christ by being living examples right in front of my eyes. But having parents who are Christians isn't enough. Nor will just being a Christian yourself guarantee a pure lifestyle, either. When I was first saved I knew something inside of me changed. Even so, I wasn't very dedicated. I still wanted to go out and have a good time with the guys.

That all changed when I met the girl who later became my wife. Her father was a pastor, but more than that, he is one of the godliest men I've ever met. Laura has three older brothers I look up to as well. All three of them love God and work in the church. Looking at Laura's family I felt like I had to step it up to win her and to show her family I was worthy of her. I couldn't coast along with a halfhearted commitment or play games with God. Even during the times we weren't dating I knew I was in love with her. To me Laura was the purest young lady I could ever imagine. I knew I wanted to marry her someday even though we were still in high school, and I never wanted to do anything that might blow that possibility.

I first made a commitment to purity because of the girl I wanted to marry, but there soon came a point where I didn't do this for her. I did it for God. Don't get me wrong. It wasn't easy. I'm a normal guy. I know how strong desires can be. But I also know we can't live our lives controlled by our desires. Once you start living your life in a certain way it develops discipline in your life. It's just like sports or anything else in life. The only way to be good at anything is to be disciplined and have a lot of determination and drive. You have to have the same approach to the Christian walk. There are no shortcuts. There's no easy way to do this. It starts with a commitment you make to God. Then you have to depend on God's strength every moment of every day.

Why Purity Matters

All of this is important to me because it is important to God. When I try to live a pure life in God's eyes, my walk with Him is much closer. I feel good going to God when I have a pure heart. The last thing I want to do is give the impression I'm somehow perfect or that I never screw up. I have. When I do, God forgives me. But, to be honest, I don't like having to go to God and ask Him to forgive me for blowing it. I don't want to let Him down. Psalm 111:10 says, "The fear of the LORD is the beginning of wisdom." I take this verse seriously. I fear God. I know my life is in His hands. I know He is a loving God, but I also know He will do whatever it takes to get our attention if we live in a way He doesn't want us to. I've seen people run from God. He gets their attention one way or another. I don't want to play that game.

Does that mean I've never compromised my convictions and placed myself in a situation where I shouldn't have been? Hardly. I'm just like you. I've made my share of mistakes. When I was eighteen, in my first year in the minor leagues, the Yankees sent me from the rookie leagues in Tampa to their Class A team in Oneonta, New York. I had only played one year of college ball when the Yankees drafted me, which made me the youngest player on the Oneonta team. Most of the other guys were twenty-one or twenty-two. My first couple of starts after I was called up didn't go too well.

After one bad game I was really down, so the other guys on the team talked me into going out with them. One of the sayings in baseball is after you've had a few bad outings you need to go out and get hammered. I guess that's what they wanted to help me do. We ended up in a nightclub which was pretty crowded. Some of the guys immediately started trying to pick up girls. I sat at a table with the rest of the team, and one of the guys bought me a beer. I didn't take one sip of it. I just sat there with it in front of me like I was drinking. I knew I didn't have any business being there, and I knew the message having that beer in front of me sent to the rest of the team. But I didn't stick with my convictions because I wanted to get some of the guys off my back.

The situation could have been really bad. I hate to think of what might have happened if I had gotten hammered. My judgment would have been impaired, and I could have made one of the worst decisions of my life and screwed up my entire future. Laura and I were dating at the time. I look back and realize I might have made some decisions which might have ruined any possibility of the two of us having a life together. I thank God He protected me even in my moment of weakness. After it was over I knew I would never compromise like that again. I don't want to screw up what God has given me.

The World Is Watching

I don't really like being in the public eye, but playing nine seasons with the New York Yankees during one of the greatest runs any team ever had put me there. The success I've enjoyed as a player, especially during the postseason, placed me in the spotlight. I know baseball fans and other players are watching me all the time, not just because I'm a pro ballplayer, but because I'm vocal about my relationship with Jesus Christ.

Obviously, if I blow up during a game and start screaming profanities at the other team or do something stupid like that, everything I say about God goes right out the window. But people don't just watch for the big things. They're also watching the little things. They watch the way I carry myself. They watch to see how I will act after I have a bad game. Everyone is good when they're doing good. The real test comes when I give up a couple of home runs and pitch poorly. People watch to see how I will react. And they're listening. Hanging out in the clubhouse with other players or shooting the breeze while shagging flies out in the outfield during batting practice, I know if the conversation goes astray I need to walk off. If I stand around listening and laughing about bad jokes, my credibility is shot.

Flaws in Your Delivery

When we talk about purity, we always have to remember that not everyone wants to see us succeed. The devil obviously wants to see us fail, but some people do as well. They'll test us and look for any weakness in our character they might exploit. I know because that's how I approach the teams I pitch against. Before every team comes in, all the pitchers on our team will go over hitting charts our scouts put together. I look at where certain players best hit fastballs, whether they like them out over the plate or down and in. I also look at charts of how a certain hitter has hit me in the past. It could be in a certain situation in the game that this guy might not be the one I want to face. I may want to face the guy in the on deck circle. I talk with my catcher and go over hitters and talk about what he would like to do in the game, what certain guys hit, what we think they will do, what counts they look for (certain pitches in certain counts). All the while we're looking for anything we can use to help get a guy out.

Other teams do the same thing to me. I had a pretty good postseason going in 2001 after being named the Most Valuable Player of the American League Championship Series. But I had a terrible World Series against the Arizona Diamondbacks, especially in Game 6. We had a chance to close out the series, but I gave up six runs and left the game in the third inning. It was the worst feeling in the world, like somebody had robbed me. What made it even worse was my stuff felt so good. I threw the ball really well, but they hit everything I threw. They were looking for the exact pitch I was throwing, like they knew what was coming. And they did. They'd studied tape of me and discovered I changed my motion slightly with my different pitches.

Doing Small Things Well

Because your enemy is looking for the same kinds of weaknesses in your character, you have to make sure you not only avoid small mistakes, but that you do all the small things that will keep you close to God. That begins with spending time with Him every day by reading your Bible and praying. I will be the first to admit that sometimes I go a week without opening my Bible, and when that happens, I am very disappointed in myself. It's not that I mean to ignore God's Word. Sometimes I just get so caught up with life that I forget. Then God gets my attention and brings me right back to it.

As you spend time with God, you need to also learn to listen for His voice. To me, the awesome thing and the amazing thing about being a Christian is just how the Holy Spirit pulls me back when I get off track. When I do something wrong He convicts me so strongly that I straighten up. You and I have to learn to listen to the Spirit's voice because He guides us into God's truth and keeps us in line with God's will. When we ignore Him we stray into sin. Our heavenly Father won't leave us like that. He will get our attention and straighten us up just like any good father.

Being involved in a good church is another small detail that will help us win our battle for purity. You're going to hear me say this many times through the course of this book. A good church where the truth is preached is vital to your walk with God. When I was growing up, my family went to church Sunday mornings, Sunday nights, and Wednesday nights. I was also very involved in our youth group. It was my life. Now that I'm an adult and I can decide for myself how involved I will be in my church, my family and I still go every chance we get. I don't go because I'm afraid God will get mad if I don't. I go because I want to. I have to. My church family and the good Bible teaching I receive there make living for Jesus much, much easier.

You need to also pay attention to the little things you let into your life. The television shows you watch have a direct impact on your thought life and your walk with God. Be careful what you let into your mind. A show doesn't have to be rated R to put chinks in your character which the enemy can exploit. The same goes for the movies you go to and the music you listen to. Pay close attention to the kinds of thoughts they plant in your mind. Ask yourself what they are doing to who you are on the inside. These may be small things, but the small stuff is where the game is won or lost.

Committing yourself to a life of purity and holiness means committing everything to God, even the smallest parts of your life. Some people say I pay attention to things that are too small to matter, but that's OK. I want to be a man of God. I don't want to do anything to let Him down. To me, purity is everything. And at the end of the day I want to feel good when I go home to be with my wife and my children after being on the road for seven or ten days. I want to know I've been true to them and true to my God.

Study Questions

- The dictionary defines *pure* as "unmixed with any other matter; free from dust and dirt; blotless, stainless." When you look at your attitudes and actions, what sort of mixture do you see between God's standards and sin? What specific elements of each do you see? What sort of concentration of each is there?

- Bob asked a question none of us can ignore: Has your heart been changed by God? Or are you, like Bob, going through the motions? Does your behavior change based on the group you are around? If so, you may be where Bob was. Go back to the end of Bob's part of chapter 3. Read through the prayer with which he ended his half of the chapter. Does it express what is in your heart? Will you pray this to God right now?

- Read 1 Kings 13:1–26. What caused the prophet to incur God's anger? How big does his "sin" sound to you? Why would God punish him for such a small thing? How are you doing with the small things in your life? Are there small areas of compromise in your commitment to purity that you pass off as no big deal? What are they? Be very specific. Remember, small flaws can produce disastrous results.

- Most people fail because they fail to do the basics. Andy talked about a few basics in the Christian life that keep us on track with God, little things like reading your Bible every day, getting involved in your church, and being careful about what you let into your life. Look over these three areas in your own life. On a scale of 1 to 10 (with 1 being the worst and 10 the best), how are you doing in each of these areas? What specific changes do you need to make in your life to improve each of these?

Guard Your Heart

CHAPTER FOUR

Beating Temptation

BOB

I love to fly-fish out West in places like Montana. I love casting the fly and watching it drift down the current. But the real thrill comes when, suddenly, the multicolored flash of a rainbow trout darts out of nowhere and strikes! And my job is carefully to set the hook. That way, regardless of his acrobatics, I've got him! He's mine!

That's very similar to the picture the Scripture gives us of how Satan uses temptation against us. Temptation is the lure of taking a God-given need and choosing to meet it in a way that God never intended. Satan throws the "fly" of temptation right in front of us. He can make it dance in front of our eyes, and of course it looks great! Everything promises to be incredible! That's what the trout must think too. The lure dangles in front of the fish, promising to taste soooooo good. The fish can't control the location of the lure, but the fish can determine whether to bite. And if he bites, the hook is set, the fish is caught, and he becomes dinner.

That's exactly the picture that the biblical writer was referring to in James 1:14 when he says, "Each person is tempted when he is drawn away [lured] and enticed [snared] by his own evil desires." Temptation plays on our desires and tries to use them to hook us and drag us away. It isn't a question of *if* we will be tempted. Temptation is inevitable. We will all face it.

Temptation may be inevitable, but it is also beatable. We don't have to take the bait. God has promised that whenever we're facing temptation He will give us a way of escape. Listen to His promise from 1 Corinthians 10:13: "No temptation has overtaken you except what is common to humanity. God is faithful and He will not allow you to be tempted beyond what you are able, but with the temptation He will also provide a way of escape, so that you are able to bear it." God will provide a way of escape. All we have to do is take it. It is our choice whether to give in or run away.

It Starts with a Choice

Any battle that has ever been won in the history of the world has been won as a result of the choices made by those waging the battle. It's no different in our own lives. Whether we win or lose depends on the choices we make! And the choices we make need to be based on what God wants for our lives. He hasn't kept His desires for us a secret. Listen to 1 Thessalonians 4:3–5, "For this is God's will, your sanctification: that you abstain from sexual immorality, so that each of you knows how to possess his own vessel in sanctification and honor, not with lustful desires, like the Gentiles who don't know God."

Avoiding sexual immorality and choosing to live a holy life are choices that will determine which way the battle for your life goes. That's why the writer of Proverbs wrote in 4:23, "Guard your heart above all else, for it is the source of life." This is the first choice we must make. We must choose to place guardrails around our hearts.

In a dramatic scene from the hit miniseries *Band of Brothers,* a soldier crawls from the base camp under enemy fire to a perimeter foxhole to relieve men who have been on guard there for hours. Finally arriving, breathless from crawling on his stomach under the hail of enemy assault, he falls into the hole with the two men he's there to relieve. Both sit with cigarettes in their hands looking in the distance.

"Hey, you clowns can head back to base camp," he tells them. "I'm here! Man, is the enemy fire hot." But neither man responds. Smoke curls from the cigarettes in their hands, but neither speaks a word. Suddenly the camera angle shifts, and it becomes apparent that both men are dead! Evidently, they'd relaxed and didn't pay close attention to the perimeter they were supposed to guard. As they let down their guards, the enemy crept up and slit their throats!

In the same way, Scripture is clear we must choose to place a guard around our hearts because our enemy, Satan, wants to take us out. So how do you build a guard around your heart? Start by filling it with the Word of God. The writer of Psalms says, "How can a young man keep his way pure? By keeping Your word. I have sought You with all my heart; don't let me wander from Your commands. I have treasured Your word in my heart so that I may not sin against You" (Psalm 119:9–11).

God's Word is much more than a bunch of rules. Everything written in the Bible is there FOR YOUR BENEFIT! Listen to what God told His people as He led them to a new life in the Promised Land: "Take to heart all these words I am giving as a warning to you today, so that you may command your children to carefully follow all the words of this law. For they are not meaningless words to you but *they are your life*" (Deuteronomy 32:46–47, emphasis added).

Choosing to fill our lives with God's Word and live by it does more than guard us from temptation. He gave us His Word to guarantee you the best life possible. But you have to choose to live it. It still comes down to your choice.

Beware: Your Hard Drive Is Vulnerable

The decision to fill your heart with God's Word is just the first of many choices you have to make in the area of your moral purity. Scripture uses the term *heart* as a representation of our entire internal being—our thoughts, our emotions, our attitudes, and our perspectives. Just like the hard drive serves as the brains of your computer and drives everything it does, so your mind serves as the brains of your life and drives everything you do. And, like a computer, what goes into it inevitably comes out of it.

Your mind has two entry ports—your eyes and your ears. What comes in radically impacts the information embedded in your thoughts, perspectives, and values. The battle with temptation starts with what you choose to let into your heart through your eyes and your ears.

Be Careful What You Hear

There's a straight shot connection between your hearing mechanism and your brain. What goes in immediately registers in the executable files of your thought life. If that is true (and it is), shouldn't we be more careful about what we let in our minds through our ears? We need to ask ourselves:

- Does my favorite music keep my mind and heart pure, or do the lyrics draw me away to compromise?
- When the guys in the locker room talk about their latest conquests, do my ears zero in like scanning radars, or do I walk away?
- When discussion with my buds turns to lewd comments, sensual descriptions of girls, and explicit sexual talk, what's my response?

- Am I filling my life with so much noise of constant sound that there's rarely any time to "be still and know that He is God," and hear Him when He's trying to speak to me or warn me?
- Whose advice do I seek and why? Are they really people who have a great walk with God, or are they people who are walking so close to the edge that I experience a certain amount of exhilaration just by following their counsel?

Remember, the only one who can put a guard on your ears is you. You can't delegate this to anybody else. It is your responsibility!

Be Careful What You See

A guy's sex drive is driven by sight and imagination. While you can't help many things that will pass across your eyes, you can definitely control what stays there. And when you let something stay in the center focus of your eyes that's sexual and sensual in nature, you're accelerating the engine of your sex drive. It won't be long before it gets out of control.

What are you training and allowing your eyes to watch? *Where* are you allowing them to go? Are your eyes habitually scanning "the landscape" (good-looking girls) to see how they measure up? And are you hoping to see a little bit more than you should to get the adrenalin rush and thrill? Let's be blunt.

- When a girl with a big chest and a loose blouse leans over to pick something up, where do your eyes go?
- When a girl's skirt rides up her leg, where are your eyes glued?
- When a good-looking woman (of any age) jogs by as you drive, what do you notice first? And how long do your eyes stay there?
- Is your favorite TV show one with extreme sexual innuendos, tight tops, sex outside of marriage, and

banter between the characters that says they live and act in a way you know is wrong?

- When your mom or girlfriend receives a *Victoria's Secret* catalog, are you more eager to see it than she is?
- What about the *Sports Illustrated Swimsuit Edition*—are you still trying to convince yourself you're getting it for the articles?

I know some of you are thinking, *Gimme a break. You're trying to tell me that even looking at magazines is wrong?* Very possibly! Read the confession of Fred Stoeker who, with Stephen Arterburn, wrote *Every Young Man's Battle.* He talks about the struggle he experienced as a teen looking through the clothing ads in the Sunday newspapers: "The models were always smiling. Always available. I loved lingering over each ad insert. *It's wrong,* I admitted to myself, *but it's such a small thing, a far cry from porn.* So I continued peering through the pages, fantasizing. Occasionally, a model reminded me of a girl I once knew, and my mind rekindled the memories of our times together."[4] Can you relate?

It's easy for us to try to pass over looking the wrong way as no big deal. We see images and storylines on television and in movies and we think, *No big deal—it's only entertainment.* But it IS a big deal. Science tells us that once sensual images are seen and absorbed, a chemical change occurs in the body system of the observer. Every guy has a hormone called epinephrine that's shot into the bloodstream when he's excited sexually. And whatever he's seeing is etched into his mind. Therefore, what we absorb in moments can last for months and years.

Maybe that's why Jason can describe the collage he had on his dorm wall made of *Playboy* foldouts. That was twenty years ago, but he can remember several of them as though it were yesterday. Or why Jim remembers vividly some escapades in the backseat with a few girls in his teen years, even though he is now striving to be happily married. But once those images are emblazoned by visualization or sexual experience, they tend to stay and keep on staying.

If that's the case, you can imagine what happens with pornography. And that becomes even scarier when today the average age for a young man to get introduced to porn is eleven. What used to require going to seedy establishments and risking the possibility of being recognized today can be easily accessed anonymously and affordably in the confines of one's own house or apartment. And no one will be the wiser.

But the effects will be devastating nevertheless. The $19-billion porn industry doesn't give a rip about you as a person. All they care about is getting you hooked, so they can get your money. They also understand that porn feeds a law of life—*the law of diminishing returns.* Are you familiar with that law? Simply put: the more you get, the less it satisfies, and the more you've got to have to get the same rush. So what starts out as a casual encounter and irregular visits to the porn site or chat room begins to get its hook in you. And having bitten, the hook gets set and keeps drawing you back. What was occasional becomes regular and what becomes regular turns addictive. And the more you see, the less you're satisfied, and the more you want to experience.

Suddenly, you're not seeing members of the opposite sex as gifted people with interesting personalities, remarkable abilities, and intriguing minds—you're just seeing them as objects to be used for your physical and emotional gratification. What started with only looks grows into absorbing fantasies. But those don't satisfy either, so the next logical step is masturbation. It's often accompanied by looking at pictures and imagining scenarios with members of the opposite sex.

The primary problem and critical challenge with masturbation is that it's driven by a thought life that sees girls as objects of fulfillment and not as special creations of the Lord with feelings and emotions to be respected and valued. Arterburn and

Stoeker describe masturbation as "primarily a symptom of uncontrolled eyes and free and racing thoughts."[5]

What's a Guy Supposed to Do?

So what does a guy do to protect himself from the culture that's saturated with sex? The answer is we do exactly what Joseph did in the Old Testament. We were first introduced to him in chapter 2. Joseph had been sold into slavery by his brothers. He found himself working for a man named Potiphar. He could have become bitter, but Joseph chose to guard his heart and to live a life that honored God.

But the sticky part happened when Potiphar's wife, very likely neglected by a workaholic husband, noticed that Joseph was handsome and buff. She decided that, because her husband was neglecting her, here was a guy who could fulfill her fantasies. So she tried to entice Joseph to hop in the sack with her. (Don't you love how the Bible doesn't tiptoe around anything, including sex?)

Think of all the justifications and excuses Joseph could have made . . .

- "Just this once won't hurt anything."
- "This is my boss's wife, and I can't say no to her."
- "Hey, I've worked hard, and I deserve some fun!"
- "No one will ever know."
- "I don't intend for anybody to get hurt."
- "What am I supposed to do with all my sexual energy? I've just gotta have some release!"

Though the Bible doesn't say, I would bet anything she dressed provocatively every chance she got. She let Joseph see some skin. Showed some cleavage. Maybe she even called for a towel while she was bathing. Because she knew, like women always have, that a man is driven by sight. And if the portals of the eyes are wide open and lingering, it's only a small step to the physical plunge.

But Joseph wouldn't give in. He told her there was no way that he could do that because his boss Potiphar had trusted him with everything he had. Nothing had been held back from him . . . *except Potiphar's wife!* And then Joseph asked the ultimate question: "How could I do such a great evil and sin against God?" (Genesis 39:9).

There's the bottom line! Joseph understood he was ultimately accountable for every one of his actions as well as every one of his thoughts to the God who had created him. And Joseph had already made his decision—obviously—so that when temptation came he knew what his response would be.

How about you?

God is watching for what you do with your mind and how you respond to impure temptation with your thoughts. He said through the prophet Jeremiah, "'Am I only a God nearby,' declares the LORD, 'and not a God far away? Can anyone hide in secret places so that I cannot see him?' declares the LORD" (Jeremiah 23:23–24 NIV). Jesus also said, "For nothing is concealed that won't be revealed, and nothing hidden that won't be made known and come to light" (Luke 8:17).

So what's the solution? It can be summed up by Romans 12:1 and 2: "Therefore, brothers, by the mercies of God, I urge you to present your bodies as a living sacrifice, holy and pleasing to God; this is your spiritual worship. Do not be conformed to this age, but be transformed by the renewing of your mind, so that you may discern what is the good, pleasing, and perfect will of God."

Remember, guys:

1. You can't be one thing on Sunday and something else Monday through Saturday. With God, there's no such thing as a "*Time* magazine lifestyle"—with separate sections devoted to sports, education, and entertainment . . . and, oh yea, faith.

2. Your primary worship doesn't just happen in a church on Sunday, but every day, when you freshly commit your life to the full lordship of Jesus Christ.

3. Don't allow any area of your life, including your thought life and what you listen to and view, to be *off limits* to God.

4. Remember that what you are today determines what you will become tomorrow. Today's decisions are the foundations of tomorrow's destiny.

5. Your mind is like a computer. Whatever goes in will inevitably come out.

6. When we live life according to God's Word we will inevitably find God's will for our lives. And we can be absolutely assured that it will always be . . .

   Good—always for our best interest and never for our harm or deficit

   Pleasing—leading to our ultimate enjoyment and fulfillment

   Perfect—unable to be improved upon.

No Free Passes

ANDY

I hate giving up walks. Nothing infuriates me more than starting an inning by giving some guy a free pass to first base, except maybe walking someone with two outs in the inning. I give up enough hits already. The last thing I want to do is make it easier for the other team to score by putting a runner on first base. In the big leagues, when you start handing out walks you're just playing with fire. And if you walk two or three batters in one inning, you aren't going to last long. You might be able to work out of a self-inflicted jam once in awhile, but most of the time you can't. They always come back to haunt you.

Some of the guys reading this right now are struggling in the area of purity because you're giving the enemy a free pass right into your life. Images and impure thoughts are doing laps in your brain and you can't make them stop. You're having trouble controlling yourself with your girlfriend and you keep pushing the envelope with her. In your heart you know what is right, and you want to do it, but it feels like everything in your mind and body is working against you.

Part of the problem may well be you've let things into your life that shouldn't be there. The movies you watch, the music you listen to, your favorite television shows, and the books and magazines you read, are all building a fire inside of you that you're having trouble keeping under control. Letting these things into your life while trying to live a pure and holy life is like me trying to get out of an inning after walking the first three batters. It can be done, but the odds are against you. Most of the time you will fail.

One of the keys to keeping yourself pure is to not give temptation any free passes into your life. You can do this by building a security system into your life to protect your heart and mind. Most people lock the doors of their houses to keep anyone from breaking in. That's how you should think of your heart and mind.

The world, your flesh, and the devil are thieves trying to get into your life to steal your integrity and destroy you. They want to ruin your testimony, foul up your future, and build a wall of sin and guilt between you and God. If you aren't careful about what you let into your life, you are in essence throwing the door of your heart open and inviting them to come right in. Why would anyone do that? Instead you need to do everything you can to protect yourself and make it easier to keep your commitment to live a pure and holy life.

Let's Start with the Obvious

The simplest way to stay out of trouble is to avoid it in the first place. I know this sounds pretty obvious, but this is the place a lot of guys mess up. My approach has always been to stay out of situations where I will be tempted. I know where Satan can get to me, so I stay as far away from those places as best I can. It's like this: If I had a problem with drinking, I wouldn't go to bars or anywhere else people are drinking. If a certain kind of show on television might make me stumble, I don't turn it on. If listening to certain songs or singers puts thoughts in my head I know shouldn't be there, I don't listen to them. The same goes with books or magazines. If something starts dragging me away from Christ, I avoid it. It's that simple.

This approach may be simple, but that doesn't mean everyone gets it. Most people get themselves into trouble by being at the wrong place at the wrong time. They think they can handle the temptation, that they are strong enough not to give in. And that's when they fall. Wouldn't it be a lot smarter to just avoid those situations to begin with? The Bible says it is. Nowhere does the Bible tell us to surround ourselves with temptation and see how long we can resist it. Instead it tells us to get away from it. In 1 Corinthians 10:13, God promises that every time we are tempted, "He will also provide a way of escape, so that you are able to bear it." The best way to escape temptation is to avoid it to begin with.

All of this was put to the test in my rookie season with the Yankees in 1995. Toward the end of the season we were having a team party. A couple of other Christian players on the team and I weren't sure if we ought to go. In baseball, team means everything, and if we didn't go to the party it would be like we were snubbing the entire team.

On the other hand, I knew what kind of stuff would probably go on at this party, stuff I didn't want to be a part of. But as a twenty-two-year-old rookie I thought I needed to show up for the team. This was one of the times I fell into the "it should be OK; let's go ahead and do it" reasoning. After all, I wouldn't have to drink or do anything else that might compromise my testimony. I figured I could just mingle around drinking a Coke. No big deal.

My friends and I walked into this party and immediately I realized we'd made a mistake. It was exactly like I knew it would be. There were things that went on that I didn't want any part of. It was a bad situation. Even though I didn't join in, I knew if I stayed I would lose my testimony to the other guys on my team. They would have seen me there and thought, *he's just like everyone else.* Being accepted by the team wasn't worth that. After about two minutes, my friends and I got out of there. Like I said before, the best way to stay out of trouble is to get away from it.

So what does this mean for you? Simply put: Don't put yourself in a place where you know you will be tempted. If your language goes down the toilet when you hang out with a group of guys, don't hang out with them. Whatever makes you stumble, avoid it.

And this also means you need to be wise in the situations you allow yourself to get into, especially in your dating life. Don't put yourself in a place where you and your girlfriend will be tempted to get carried away. A good rule of thumb is this: if her parents aren't home, don't go over to her house. Bottom line, if you are by yourself with your girlfriend and no one is around and you start kissing on each other, one thing is going to lead to another even when you don't mean for it to. Don't put yourself in a place where you know you will be tempted. As long as you are around adults, and as long as you are around other people, you know you can't get away with anything. Keeping your commitment to purity is much easier if you simply avoid places where you will be tempted.

Fill Your Heart with Scripture

If you want to keep your life on track, listen to and obey the Bible. Philippians 4:8–9 tell us how: "Finally brothers, whatever is true, whatever is honorable, whatever is just, whatever is pure, whatever is lovely, whatever is commendable—if there is any moral excellence and if there is any praise—dwell on these things. Do what you have learned and received and heard and seen in me, and the God of peace will be with you." If you want God to be with you, fix your thoughts on His Word. Read it and think about it throughout your day. That's what this verse is talking about. And don't just think about what the Bible says. Obey it. Do what it says. I know, this is obvious as well. None of this is rocket science. It is all pretty basic. Yet the basics are where most people mess up.

What I try to do is this: I wake up in the morning and start my day with my Bible. When I was in high school I would always get some sort of devotional book because, to me, that was easier than just opening up the Bible and reading. Good devotionals help relate the verses you read to your life, then you can go and look them up in your Bible. Not only do I try to start my day with the Bible, I also get into the Word in my church. My father-in-law is the pastor of our church and an excellent preacher. His sermons make the Bible come alive and help me put it into action in my life.

I also believe a good way to get the Bible into your life is by surrounding yourself with it. My favorite verse is Philippians 4:13, "I can do all things through Christ who strengthens me" (NKJV). I take this verse with me out onto the mound every time I pitch. I don't use it to try to convince God to let me win the game. Instead the verse reminds me that I can face any challenge I may face through Christ. Every time I pitch I want to represent God. This verse helps me do that. It is so important to me that I had it painted on the floor of my gym where I do my off-season workouts. In the center of the gym is a baseball with a cross in it and these words, "I can do all things through Christ who strengthens me."

I'm no one special. This promise isn't just for me. *You* can do anything through Christ who gives you strength. And one of the main ways He gives us strength is through His Word. The Bible says it is our spiritual food. If you are weak and about to fold under the pressure of temptation, it could be you haven't been eating like you should. Get back into the Word. It's one of your best lines of defense.

Don't Play with Fire

One of the questions guys always ask when the conversation turns to purity is "How far is too far?" They want to know how far they can go physically with their girlfriends or how far they can push the envelope with their language or what types of movies they can go see. I've got to tell you, when you start plotting how much you can get away with, you're already setting yourself up for trouble.

When I face a guy like Alex Rodriguez or Manny Ramirez, players who've had a lot of success against me in the past, I'm not thinking about how many pitches down the middle of the plate I can get away with. No, all I care about is getting out of the inning without giving up any runs. If we have a two-run lead and I have an open base, I'm not going to give these guys anything to hit. I'll try to get them to chase stuff out of the strike zone, and if they happen to walk, I'm OK with that. As an athlete I have a lot of pride, but sometimes I have to swallow my pride. In the middle of the game I'm more concerned about getting out of the inning than proving I can win a showdown with Manny Ramirez. I'll happily let him go to first base when I know I have a much better chance of getting out the next hitter. I'm not going to mess around and play with fire.

That's how you and I have to approach living a pure and holy life. Ephesians 5:3 (NIV) tells us to avoid even the hint of immorality. That means that rather than trying to figure out how far you can push the envelope, you need to do everything you can to keep away from sin. So how do you know when you've crossed the line into a "hint of immorality"? With language I think it's pretty simple: can you imagine Jesus using the words you do or telling the jokes you enjoy? With girls I think when your mind gets out of control and starts fantasizing about going further, you've gone too far. And that doesn't just apply to the girls you date. If a girl walks by and you start undressing her in your mind, you've jumped into sin. Even if you haven't done anything physically, you've already committed immorality in your heart and mind.

This whole question goes beyond how much you can get away with before you cross the line into impurity. The Bible tells us that sin starts in our minds. God holds us accountable for the thoughts on which we dwell. Jesus Himself said, "Everyone who looks at a woman to lust for her has already committed adultery with her in his heart" (Matthew 5:28).

So how far is too far when it comes to a physical relationship with a girl? I'd say it is whenever lust begins. For some of you, you may not be able to kiss your girlfriend because you want to do something else. And you also have to think about the girl you're dating. Passionate kisses create a spark in her that makes her want to go a little further. When that happens you're playing with fire. And when you play with fire, you always get burned.

Set limits for yourself. Figure out what you can and cannot control. Listen, I can't give you some rule like "never kiss a girl." You have to grow up and figure out some things for yourself. Part of this is obvious. When your hands start roaming you've obviously crossed a line God doesn't want crossed. But even if you can control your hands, you have to learn to control your mind.

One of the best ways I've found to do this is to get busy doing something else. Play sports and work to become the best you can be. If you aren't into sports, play a musical instrument or do something that will occupy your time and keep your mind from focusing on girls all the time. Second Corinthians 10:5 tells us to take our every thought captive and make it obedient to Jesus Christ. When we let our minds run wild, we set ourselves up for failure.

Depend on God's Grace to Carry You Through

Ultimately, the greatest protection you have in your life is God's grace. Honestly, as I look back on my life I don't know how I am able to keep my commitment to purity except that God does it. I didn't always see it back when I was younger, but I now understand that God's hand was on me. His grace not only protected me from bad situations; He also protected me from myself. One of the ways God did this in my life was through my parents and my wife's parents. They prayed for us constantly while we were dating. Their prayers kept God's hand on Laura and me. And the prayers of my friends and family are still vital to me today. I know the reason I can honor God when I step up on the pitcher's mound is because so many people pray for me every day.

First Corinthians 10:13 gives us this promise: "No temptation has overtaken you except what is common to humanity. God is faithful, and He will not allow you to be tempted beyond what you are able, but with the temptation He will also provide a way of escape, so that you are able to bear it." God has always kept this promise to me, and He will to you as well. When temptation strikes, look around. God will provide an escape hatch to let you get away. You need to use it, even when you don't feel like it.

This takes us back to what we talked about in the first chapter. The key to living a life of purity is to live your life for the Lord. Fill your life with Him. Learn everything you can about

Him. Worship Him. Obey Him. Love Him. I've found it is a lot easier to live for Christ when I'm around other Christians. You will too. That's why you need to get involved in a church. When I was a teenager, the youth department in our church was a huge part of my life. Find a group in which you can grow spiritually. Get involved. Serve God there. Resisting temptation is a lot easier when you focus all of your attention on serving Christ.

Living a life of integrity will never be easy. But in the end, it is worth it.

Study Questions

- Temptation plays on the desires that are already inside of us. How then can you guard your heart from temptation's appeal? How does this relate to what you allow to enter your heart and mind through your eyes and your ears? What does the music you listen to or the movies you watch have to do with the desires temptation plays upon? Bob talked about this in general terms, but now it is time for you to take a hard look at your own life. How does the music *you* listen to and the movies *you* watch affect your thought life and the desires dwelling inside of you?

- Bob and Andy both quote 1 Corinthians 10:13. Look this verse up in your Bible and underline it. Look closely at the last phrase, "He will also provide a way of escape." What does this mean and how does this affect the way you resist temptation? How can you recognize the "way of escape"?

- Andy talked about guarding your heart by filling it with Scripture. What is the difference between reading the Bible and having it fill your heart? Have you ever tried doing this? If so, what kind of results did you see? Why does this even matter?

- Ephesians 5:3 (NIV) tells us to avoid even the hint of immorality. That means each one of us must figure out our own vulnerabilities and set limits for ourselves. It was easy to read about this. Now it is time to do it. Look over the three areas of purity where you struggle the most. What kinds of limits do you need to set for yourself to keep yourself from crossing the line? If you didn't include your dating life, think about it now. Write out some specific guidelines you will follow. And remember, the key to success is God's grace, not your willpower.

Indispensable Ingredients for a Pure and Holy Life

CHAPTER FIVE

A Walk That Matches Your Talk

BOB

I'd never seen that view of the hallway at my high school and for good reason—I'd never been *inside* a locker! But that's where Jeff shoved me on a day I'll never forget.

Here's what happened. Jeff and I were in an honors chemistry class together. Our teacher, Mr. McClary, had been out of school for several weeks due to a heart attack. During his absence, an exam had rolled around—and my study for it had been pretty much zip. Instead of studying I had a good time.

On Monday, when the exam hit, I only had to read the first question to know I was in deep trouble! When you're drowning and going down for the third time, what do you do? You reach for a life preserver! And mine was Randy, the class brain who sat next to me. I nudged him and let him know I needed help. Out of friendship, he scooted his paper over so I could see it and the test became a community project.

With his help I was flying through the exam when suddenly, as I bent over my desk writing furiously, I noticed some shoes had appeared in my line of vision on the floor. I immediately knew they weren't mine because they pointed in exactly the opposite direction. We were busted by the substitute teacher. He took our tests, ripped them up, and told us he would report the incident to Mr. McClary who was returning in a week. Getting caught cheating would mean an automatic *F* in the class, along with a possible suspension, and an exploding father. I can't tell you how much I sweated during that week.

On Mr. McClary's first day back, he called Randy and me into his office and asked for the truth. Now you need to understand that Randy and I knew we were Mr. McClary's "pets." So I looked at the teacher and, rather than answering his question, asked my own: "Mr. McClary, do you *really* think Randy and I would do such a thing?"

The teacher looked us in the eye, then a smile broke across his face, and he said, "I *knew* you guys wouldn't cheat. So I'm going to give you the exam again." Then he handed us a makeup test and told us to take it in an empty room down the hall—together—without anyone watching us. Can you believe it? We'd been caught red-handed cheating once, and now our teacher gave us a golden opportunity to do it again! And we did, I'm sad to say.

Which brings me back to Jeff and the locker. He'd been watching the whole thing. He knew I went to church, and he was trying to find out if church really made a difference in anybody's life. After I cheated my way through the makeup exam, Jeff grabbed me in the hall and crammed me into an open locker. He slammed the door shut and sneered, "I was told you were different because you are a Christian. But I know all about the chemistry test! The fact is, you aren't any different than me! So much for the Jesus you say you follow!"

Staring out at Jeff's angry face through the vent slots in the top of the locker door a sick feeling swept over me. It would be a few years before I realized I didn't really know Jesus Christ personally at that time but had only been going through the motions. I'd equated being a church member with being a Christ-follower—and the two are *not* equal! No matter what I said I believed, Jeff had found me out. My walk didn't come close to matching my talk! I lacked integrity, and it cost me all my credibility in Jeff's eyes.

That's what integrity is all about. It's a commodity that people thirst to see and desire above all else to find in people in whom they put their trust. They want integrity to characterize their relationships with friends, the opposite sex, business partners, and the leaders they follow.

What exactly is integrity? Here's a working definition: *Integrity, for the Christian, is absolute harmony between what God's Word requires, what the Christ-follower believes, and what his actions and attitudes prove.* The bottom line: God expects our walk to match our talk! What ingredients make that happen? Let's take a look at a man in Scripture who had integrity in spades—Joshua. And let's look at what made him walk with integrity all the days of his life.

Asking for Directions

Joshua is the main character in the book of the Bible that bears his name. He led the armies of Israel in their greatest battles as they conquered the land God promised to give them four hundred years earlier. You would think someone with that kind of résumé would have a little strut to his step. Anyone else in that position may get an attitude that screams, "Hey, look at me!" but Joshua's character reflected a simple word called *humility*.

Humility is a willingness to look to others to help you become the very best you can be. It's understanding you don't have everything on your own that you need to accomplish all that God put you here to do and to be. That takes a Big Man, regardless of his age.

Take a look at Joshua. As gifted, talented, and equipped as he was, what you find him doing for years is serving somebody else—namely Moses. For more than forty years, long before anyone put him in charge of anything, Joshua put himself in the role of an intern, taking advantage of every opportunity to learn all he could from Moses. One of the great strengths of a guy who truly has it together is recognizing people who can teach him how to be better in areas of his life. He's constantly looking for ways to improve, stretch, strengthen, and deepen his abilities, character, and impact. But it takes a humble guy to do that.

I've noticed through the years that when I find a guy who struts with cockiness as though he's got the world by the tail, he may succeed for awhile. He may impress girls in the short run or be seen as cool—but give it time. The self-centeredness gets old. The lack of sensitivity for those around him wears thin. The attempt to be the world's Answer Man leaves everybody gasping for relief. But find a guy humble enough to build on his good qualities with the help of mentors, and you'll find a guy who will make a lasting difference.

Humility expresses itself in three critical qualities. A humble man is faithful, available, and teachable.

Faithful

A man who's humble will be faithful in doing whatever task he's charged with accomplishing. He won't just do it part way or with frustrated reluctance. He'll do it to the very best of his ability, whatever that is. He won't get started on a job and then decide he's had enough and quit. He'll see it to the finish. These guys go the extra mile.

- In sports, they'll be at practice earlier, work harder, and stay longer than others on the team.

- In music, they'll be more focused in their practice and do the scales until they're sick of running notes, knowing if they master the basics, the rest will come easier.
- At school they'll wisely choose times to say no when the rest of the gang wants to go running around even though a test is closing in. They know the time sacrificed for study now will pay off in huge dividends in good grades and the doors those grades will open later.
- At home taking care of the yard for mom and dad, they won't just mow it, they'll trim it and bag the trimmings too.

Being faithful is what Jesus meant when He said, "Whoever can be trusted with very little can also be trusted with much, and whoever is dishonest with very little will also be dishonest with much" (Luke 16:10 NIV).

Available

The guy who's humble will always be available to help. He will go out of his way to support others in their endeavors and not just look out for his own. When he sees a need, his response is, "Somebody needs to do something about that" and HE is that somebody!

Being available is the spirit Isaiah expressed when he encountered God in Isaiah 6. He heard God's need for someone to go and tell others about Him. What was Isaiah's response? *Here am I, send me!* Too many of us respond with something more like, "Here am I, . . . send him!" The guy who's available will see a need and offer *himself* to fill it.

Teachable

The humble guy is always willing to listen to somebody with more experience. His eyes don't roll when his dad tries to give him advice. He doesn't float into a coma when a teacher tries to help him improve in an area or skill. He doesn't respond with resentment to people who are further in their journey of life than he is and are interested in helping him reach his fullest potential.

Instead, the teachable guy doesn't just wait to learn from others; he seeks out others from whom he can learn. He's always looking for someone he respects and admires and then seeks opportunities to learn everything he can from them. The benefit of their experience helps him grow significantly into what God created him to be.

Faithful, available, and *teachable*—these three words describe Joshua. For almost forty years, he served Moses rather than looking to be served. Somehow he grasped that in God's perspective *those who are going to be greatest are those who are committed to serving others.* Listen to what Jesus said centuries later: "Whoever wants to become great among you must be your servant, and whoever wants to be first among you must be your slave; just as the Son of Man did not come to be served, but to serve, and to give His life—a ransom for many" (Matthew 20:26–28).

The Only Way to Play Is by the Book!

When you play sports, you become familiar with the playbook. It describes how to execute plays which, when done in excellence and with consistency, will produce a winning outcome. The playbook becomes like a bible in the sport. It's the rule for life, and for play, for the athlete when he's on the field or the court or the diamond.

The playbook in sports exists for one purpose—to guide the team to victory. That's exactly God's intent for your life and mine and why He gave us the Bible. He had no intention of the Bible being a killjoy in our lives, keeping us from fun, fulfillment, or a great future. Just as the tracks on a roller coaster are there to keep you from careening out of control so you can enjoy the ride, God gave His Word to make our lives the best they can be.

In 2 Timothy 3:16–17, God assures us that *every single word of the Bible is true.* Listen to what it says, "All Scripture is inspired by God and is profitable for teaching, for rebuking, for correcting, for training in righteousness, so that the man of God may be complete, equipped for every good work." These words are a promise from God. If we live by His Word it will guide us in how we should live, bring to our attention those times we're not living for God, correct us and get us back on the right track, and help us to stay there. Then He concludes the two verses with an amazing promise. He says when we live by the guidelines found in God's Owner's Manual for our lives, we will be thoroughly equipped for every good thing God brings our way!

Joshua learned to play by the Book. In the first chapter of Joshua, God told him very clearly to make sure that he knew what the Book said and the instructions God provided in it for effective living. God said His Word was so important it should become a daily part of Joshua's life, and he should be thinking constantly, day and night, about the guidelines He gives for dynamic living (Joshua 1:8–9). And if Joshua would do that, God made another amazing promise. He said Joshua would be successful in whatever he did. The context indicates that Joshua's success would be in making great and wise decisions that would help him fulfill his mission and purpose in life. How are you doing in that?

If not so well, are you regularly getting into the Word of God? And is the Word of God getting into you?

An Indispensable Quality

To be a man of integrity also requires a quality that's a key ingredient to be successful in anything in life. Maybe you can guess what it is.

- What quality does a big league pitcher want every time he steps onto the mound?

- What does a hitter want every time he steps up to the plate?
- What does an NFL quarterback want every time he walks onto the football field?
- What quality do you hope the doctor has when you're ill?
- What do you want every time you get in your car to go somewhere?

The answer is *CONSISTENCY.* We need to count on things working and people around us who are consistent—at the top of their profession and game. An effort to be consistent is a critical part of integrity. Remember: Integrity, for the Christian, is absolute harmony between what God's Word requires, what the Christ-follower believes, and what his actions and attitudes prove. We learn that we can depend on what's consistent, but we can't depend on what's not. That's true with equipment, repetitive occurrences, and, yes, even people.

Even society has a desire to see consistency between claims, expectations, and actions. Former Baylor University basketball coach Dave Bliss was at the top of his game until the summer of 2003. He'd been honored five times as his Conference's Coach of the Year and he'd coached seven Conference championship teams. Eleven of his players had gone on to be NBA draft picks.

But as respected as Dave Bliss was, evidence surfaced that he'd tried to cover up an unethical tuition payment to Patrick Dennehy. Then, when Dennehy was found slain, Bliss asked Dennehy's teammates and the team's assistant coaches to lie to investigators—to say that apparently Dennehy had gotten the money selling drugs. The abuses in the Baylor basketball program were revealed after Dennehy's disappearance from campus on June 12, 2003. His body was found outside Waco on July 25, and a former teammate, Carlton Dotson, was arrested in Maryland and charged with shooting his friend to death.

Bliss had been guilty of giving money under the table to Dennehy and then trying to cover it up. Dennehy's stepfather said of Bliss, "He was at the memorial service, and I shook his hand. That two-faced jerk! And he's supposed to be such a religious man from such a religious school!"[6] Bliss had evidently paid the school's $17,000 tuition when he discovered his star basketball player's family couldn't afford it, and the athlete didn't qualify for financial aid. He scrambled to cover it up. Finally, on August 8, he admitted to Baylor officials that he'd personally made tuition payments to two players, not only one. The result: a respected coach who said all the right things was thrown out of his job because his walk didn't match his talk!

This is the very kind of thing Jesus meant when He warned those who claimed to follow Him, saying, "This people honor Me with their lips, but their heart is far from Me. They worship Me in vain, teaching as doctrines the commands of men" (Mark 7:6–7).

God told Joshua that he was to get into the Book of the Law (God's Word) and let it be a guide to his life "so that you may carefully observe everything written in it" (Joshua 1:8). God commanded Joshua to be consistent—his attitudes and actions were to match instructions for living found in His Word.

How are you doing in that? Is there consistency between God's guidelines for living and your beliefs, your attitudes, and your actions?

It Takes Courage

Let's be honest—being a committed Christian guy isn't always easy. We can't help but think: *What will the other guys say? Will they want to hang with me anymore? Will they think I'm a loser?* Isn't it interesting that we always focus first on what everybody else will think instead of what God will think?

Living a faith-based life is never easy. It takes courage and boldness. It requires taking risks and launching out on an adventure. It's for guys who aren't satisfied with being in some-body else's mold but want to be men who make a difference in life. They want to make their lives count!

That's why God said to Joshua three different times in Joshua 1, "Be strong and courageous!" Because He said it three times in such a very short space, do you think He was trying to get a message across? I think He was saying this is where we separate the men from the boys. Do they have the courage to step out and follow Me? asks God. Or will they be content with saying the right things but missing the right way of walking?

Isn't that what Jesus meant when He said, "Not everyone who says to Me, 'Lord, Lord!' will enter the kingdom of heaven, but [only] the one who does the will of My Father in heaven" (Matthew 7:21). And, "Why do you call Me 'Lord, Lord,' and don't do the things I say?" (Luke 6:46).

Now that you've looked at Joshua's life, and lined it up next to your own, let's ask a question: Does your walk match your talk—or do you have some work to do?

Help along the Way

ANDY

In my last season with the Yankees, we started it off at a blis-tering pace. We blew through the month of April with the best record in baseball, 21–6. Sportswriters started comparing us to our 1998 team that won 114 games and swept the World Series. But everything changed in the month of May. The team struggled and I struggled. We started giving up a lot of runs and losing games, especially at Yankee Stadium. Even though it was still early in the season we knew we needed to find a way to turn things around but nothing seemed to work.

It was bad enough that the team was struggling, but I couldn't find a way to help. After going 4–1 in April, I lost my first three starts in May. I'd never lost more than two in a row in my entire career and suddenly I was sitting on three straight losses. I wasn't alone. The other guys on the pitching staff were inconsistent, our bats were cold, and our fielding left a lot to be desired. As a team we were playing poorly. But that happens in a long season. Usually when the team struggles I just think to myself, *Big deal, overcome it. If the team isn't scoring runs, throw a shutout if you have to, but do whatever it takes to help the team get back on track.*

That's usually how I handle these kinds of situations. But going into my fourth start of May after losing three games in a row I was thinking, *OK, if no one else is going to do something to turn this thing around, if no one else is going to turn in a good effort, then I will have to do it myself.* It was the first game of a three-game home series against the Toronto Blue Jays, a team we swept in the first four games of the season in their ballpark. Going into the game I decided I would throw as hard as I could and blow these guys away.

Before I knew it I was four batters into the game and I was behind three to nothing. My velocity was up more than ninety-three miles per hour, but they were hitting the ball out of the park. When I tried to win the game by myself I got away from everything that makes me successful as a pitcher. Usually I try to stay nice and relaxed no matter what happens. I know the team is backing me, and I trust my catcher knows what he is doing when he puts a sign down for a pitch. But in this game against the Blue Jays I got away from all of that, and I got lit up.

My manager, Joe Torre, pulled me in the fourth inning after I'd given up nine hits and seven runs. I had five strikeouts, not that it mattered. Walking off the field the competitor inside of me was embarrassed. But sometimes embarrassing things happen in our lives. I had to go back to the very basics. I had to come back to God and say to Him, "You're going to make me have a nervous breakdown here because I can't figure this out. But You also told me You wouldn't put more on me than I can handle, so help me figure out how to handle this."

For me, everything comes back to God. I know I can't do anything on my own. Trying to do things by myself doesn't work. My season turned around when I quit focusing on myself and went back to doing things God's way. I know I need to do everything I can to get ready to pitch. Working out every day, watching videotape, studying hitting charts, meeting with my catcher to discuss hitters, these are my part of the equation. But I also know that I have to rely completely on the Lord in everything I do.

If I can't be successful throwing a baseball relying on my ability alone, why would any of us think we could live a life that honors God on our own? Yet that's exactly what we often end up doing. We think living a life of purity comes down to nothing more than us saying no to sex outside of marriage. But there is so much more to it than that. As we've already talked about, living a life of purity means honoring God with every part of your life. You can't do that on your own. You need help. And that help starts with God.

Depending on God

The key to living a pure and holy life is to constantly grow closer and closer to the Lord. It isn't enough to make rules for yourself of what you *won't* do. You need more than vowing to wait until you are married to have sex or never taking a drink of alcohol or not watching movies with a lot of sex in them. You need a real, growing walk with Christ where you depend on Him completely. This is where a lot of guys trip up. They think, *I was close to God once. That's good enough.* But it isn't.

When I was growing up, my buddies and I would all go off to church camp every summer. While we were there a bunch of the guys would all get saved, but then we would go back to school and they wouldn't want anything to do with church. Then I would invite them to winter camp, and they would go and have the greatest trip of their lives. They would all rededicate their lives to Christ and be all serious about God again. But then we would go back to school and the cycle would repeat itself. They wanted the spiritual highs instead of a daily walk with the Lord.

That may be where you are. You live for those little highs and you think that is enough. Then we start talking about purity, and you think those spiritual highs will carry you through. But they won't.

We have to constantly strive to get closer and closer to the Lord and depend on Him completely. It isn't easy. I screw up here so much myself. I get complacent with where I am spiritually and suddenly, just after a day or two, I find I'm far away from God. Thankfully the Lord always comes along and hits me on my forehead to wake me up. He's constantly saying, "What are you doing, Andy. Let's go." And that's what makes me want to get closer to Him. Being close to God is like going to the World Series. I've pitched some great games there, but that's not enough. I want to go back. The same is true of my relationship with God. It isn't enough to have been close to Him once. I want to grow closer to Him today.

Learning from the Wisdom of Others

We can't do anything apart from Christ. That is a given. Yet God usually doesn't just drop the help we need down out of the sky. He works in our lives through people, especially the people who care the most about us. And those are the people we need around us if we are to win this battle for purity in our lives. Not only do we need the grace and strength only God can supply; we need the wisdom and guidance of our parents, our pastors, and other Christians who have walked this path before us.

In 1996 I won twenty-one games in only my second year in the major leagues. At the time I don't think I really appreciated how many factors beyond my control had to come together to make this possible. Some great pitchers go their entire careers without ever winning twenty games once. At the end of that season our pitching coach, Mel Stottlemyre, came to me and told me my life would never be the same. He told me how the organization and the fans would expect me to win twenty every season. Mel knew what I could expect because he'd been through it himself. In 1965 he won twenty games for the Yankees in his second season in the majors. I listened to Mel and took his advice because he'd walked this same road before me.

This is how God works. He puts people in your life for a reason. Your parents and your pastor and the other adult Christian leaders around you know what you are going through. Learn from them. Some of them may have messed up in the area of purity when they were your age, but that doesn't mean they don't have anything to say. If they messed up, learn from their mistakes. The thing is to be teachable. Surround yourself with good people. These are the ones you should listen to. That's how you learn. That's how you grow.

That doesn't mean learning from them will be easy. During my nine seasons with the Yankees, I often came into the dugout between innings and Mel told me what I was doing wrong on the mound. There were times I wanted to argue with him and tell him to leave me alone because I knew what I was doing. But when I listened instead of fighting, I found he knew what he was talking about. In the heat of the battle or when you are under stress, it is hard to listen to people, but you have to if you are going to succeed. I've played with guys who had a little bit of success in the past and stopped trying to get better. They won't listen to the coaches or the other players when all they want to do is help them get better. Those guys don't last very long, not on a winning team.

Sometimes we don't listen because of who is trying to give us advice. We have a tendency to not listen when it's our mom or dad trying to tell us something. When Mel tells me something I listen, but if my dad told me the same thing I would have a tendency to dismiss it just because it is my dad. You may be the same way. Instead of automatically dismissing everything my father says, or getting mad at him for trying to tell me what to do, I need to listen. I know he's looking out for my best interests.

Accountability

Not only do you need to learn from the wisdom of others, you also need to surround yourself with friends who will help keep you on track. I've always tried to latch onto someone who would hold me accountable. I think it is very important to find someone who is solid and try to hang with him to help keep your life on line.

When I was a rookie our best relief pitcher, John Wettland, took me under his wing. He was a veteran ballplayer who had a solid walk with God. Not only did he help me become a part of the team; he helped me see what it meant to live for Christ in the big leagues. After John left the Yankees following our 1996 World Series title, God brought outfielder Chad Curtis into my life. During our three years as teammates I found Chad to be as solid in his Christian faith as anyone I've ever played with or been around. He's a guy who has a lot of wisdom and Bible knowledge. Not only that, Chad is a deep thinker and he challenged me in some areas of my life I'd never even thought about before. Just being around him was a learning experience for me. He not only helped me live a life of purity and integrity; he helped me get to know God better.

Of course, there were times Chad would get under my skin. He had this way of dropping little hints when he wanted to make a point. During road trips we would get on a plane and I would plug in a DVD movie, put on my headphones, and sit back and relax. But Chad would come up to me and some of the other Christian guys on the team and say, "Hey guys, we're Christian brothers here; let's get together and talk." To be honest, I just wanted to sit there and enjoy the movie, but he would say, "Whatever you are doing in your life, you are either doing one of two things. You are either going up for God or you are going down from God. One way or the other." Then he would ask if God would rather have us sit there and watch that movie, or would He rather us talk about the Lord.

When Chad did this, part of me wanted to tell him to shut up and leave me alone. But he wasn't trying to make me mad. He had my best interests at heart. And when I stopped and thought about it I realized he was right. I threw away half of my DVDs because of him. He made me look at parts of my life I wouldn't have otherwise.

We all need friends like this. Through the years God has given me teammates like Chad Curtis, Scott Brosius, Sterling Hitchcock, Chris Hammond, and Lance Berkman—guys who love the Lord and have made me a stronger believer. He doesn't just bring people like this into the life of Andy Pettitte. Look around. I've always found God is faithful to put people in our lives we can draw strength from and grow closer to God with.

But for people like this to touch your life you have to be willing to learn from them. That takes a lot of humility. I've found purity and humility go hand in hand. You can't have one without the other. The Bible says pride comes before a fall (Proverbs 16:18). That simply means when we get full of ourselves we will end up making fools of ourselves. Humility does just the opposite. It forces us to listen even when we don't want to.

A Team Effort

Living a life of purity is a team effort. You can't do this by yourself. I know I couldn't. No one can. And one of the most important people you need to have on your team are the girls you date. They must have the same commitment to purity. If you are thinking about dating someone who doesn't, don't date her.

I started dating the girl who is now my wife when I was fifteen and she was thirteen. We dated a very long time before we married. Both of us believed sex before marriage is wrong, and we were committed to living a life of purity. That doesn't mean I wasn't tempted or that keeping the physical part of our relationship under control was a piece of cake. I'm a guy just like you. Thoughts fly through our heads and temptation hits. But Laura's commitment to purity made me stronger. If it wasn't for her I don't know that I could have controlled myself.

I can't tell you how important this is. Remember, living a pure and holy life isn't just about refraining from having sex until you say "I do." It means living a life that honors God in everything you do. This is what God wants from every one of us. That's why the Bible tells us not to be unequally yoked (2 Corinthians 6:14). The girls you date must have the same commitment to Christ and honoring Him. Without it they will pull you away from God.

So how can you know if that girl you have your eye on has the same commitment to Christ and purity? Ask her. Laura and I talked about this constantly when we were dating. All of us talk about the things that are most important to us. If purity matters, talk about it.

Sharing a commitment to purity will change the way you date. It will keep you from putting yourself in a situation you will not be able to handle. Listen, everyone—no matter how strong their faith and how firm their commitment to Christ—can be tempted and end up doing things they never thought they would do. I doubt if King David expected to find himself sending for another man's wife so he could sleep with her. But he did, and the results were disastrous. If a guy who wrote parts of the Bible can fall, so can you.

You and your girlfriend might have the best of intentions, but if you go over to her house after school alone, when her parents won't be home for hours, you may well find things will get out of hand. So don't put yourselves in a situation where you will be tempted. Be very careful about kissing in the swimming pool or anything else that makes your mind start racing toward moving things to a new level. When you find yourself being tempted, stop. Also, do things with a group and pray at the beginning of dates. I've even heard of couples who would place a Bible between them while they were driving on a date or sitting and watching television. Your girl might find these kinds of actions very strange, unless she has the same commitment to a pure life. And whenever either of you find yourselves getting carried away, especially in your thought life, end the date and leave.

Again, I cannot stress how important this is. Your commitment to a pure and holy life doesn't just affect you. It also touches the lives of every girl you will ever date and the men they will eventually marry. That's why the girls you ask out must have the same commitment to Christ and holiness. You need to think of them as a part of your team. No one can win the game by themselves. Your success depends on them as much as yourself. You can't do this alone.

Study Questions

- Does your walk match your talk? How consistent is your Christian life? In what areas of your life are you most consistent? Where are you least consistent? Does a lack of consistency ever make you wonder why you should even keep trying? How can you overcome this? What does your desire to do better say about the work God is doing in your life?

- Bob started the chapter with a story about when he blew his testimony big time. If you put yourself in a similar situation, what then should you do? How can you be faithful, available, and teachable in the midst of a situation where you've just compromised your integrity and other people know it?

- Purity is far more than saying no to sin. The key to living a life that honors God in everything we do is to depend on Him in all that you do. How can you move this from being an idea in a book to a daily reality in your life? What are some tangible ways you can express your dependence on God and find the help from Him you need?

- Who has God placed in your life to help you on your journey toward purity? What do you see in their character you need in your own life? Read Ecclesiastes 4:9–12. Having someone there to pick you up when you fall is part of accountability; that is, having a team of guys who can help you on your journey toward purity. Find someone in your youth group or at school with whom you can build an accountability relationship. Write their names down here. Meet with them this week to discuss holding one another accountable in your walk with Christ and your commitment to purity.

Going against the Flow

CHAPTER SIX

Swimming Upstream

BOB

Christened as the most luxurious and *unsinkable* ship that ever sailed, the *Titanic* left England for America in 1912. Several days into its maiden voyage, in the black of night on April 14, the unsinkable ship sank to the bottom of the ocean in only three hours.

Decades later, when the ship's carcass was discovered on the ocean floor, experts learned how the tragedy happened. The ocean liner had lost a battle with its enemy, an iceberg, just below the waterline. It turns out that the steel used to build it was of inferior quality, and it became brittle in the North Atlantic's frigid waters. When the knife-sharp ice penetrated the brittle hull, watertight compartments began to flood, more compartments than the ship's designers ever anticipated, thus destroying the ship's buoyancy.

No one associated with the *Titanic* expected the tragedy that would take so many passengers and crew to their icy grave.

Engineers and promoters claimed it was unsinkable. Newspapers claimed "Even God Couldn't Sink the *Titanic!*" so no one bothered to question why it wasn't equipped with enough lifeboats and vests.

On the night it was struck, the ship was going too fast for such treacherous waters. The radio room had failed to take heed of at least six warnings telegraphed by other ships that knew about icebergs in the area. And the ultimate danger was not above the waterline, where lookouts could see it, but below. It was a chunk of ice broken off from an iceberg with nine-tenths of its mass hidden beneath the water's surface.

That's how a lot of experiences in life happen. We sail along and are suddenly struck by dangers lurking beneath the surface. Because we think we're invincible (unsinkable), we ignore the warnings and plunge full-speed ahead. When tragedy strikes, we sink to the bottom of our own private ocean.

Jeremy was like that. He attended his church's youth group and led an early morning Bible study at school. He and his girlfriend, Shawna, had vowed not to have sex. Both were headed for college.

Jeremy was so sure of his ability to resist evil that he decided to do some Internet surfing, looking online for nonbelievers whom he could tell about Christ. It was a noble idea. He found one chat room, then another and another. He seemed to have tapped into some weird group who liked to write about their sexual fantasies. He shared Christ with a few, but they blew him off. Still, he tried. Night after night, Jeremy went online.

Shawna noticed he had less time for her. His best buddy, Tyrone, began wondering what was up. Jeremy seemed withdrawn, and he wasn't sharing his prayer requests anymore. Jeremy claimed he was spending more time hitting the books. With college next year, that made sense. But his nights were becoming more devoted to going online, looking for the fantasy groups.

Jeremy began blogging. His journal recorded his own thoughts, and some of them were pretty raw. He figured he wasn't hurting anybody. One night he linked to somebody else's blog, then another and another. He found out what a small world it was when a hyperlink from one of the fantasy groups led to his own blog and tied him to the Bible study he led with Tyrone at school. Soon his credibility was at stake and so was his position of leadership. His youth pastor found out. So did his parents. And so did Shawna, who thought he was becoming more aggressive on their dates. Jeremy was sinking fast.

How did it happen? Jeremy went off on his own, trying to "minister" to a very tough crowd without accountability to his prayer partner and friend. He overestimated his strength. He tapped into the world of sexual fantasies and was sucked in. It seemed safe at first, but it became seductive. Jeremy got in over his head and began to drown.

Learn to See the Hidden Dangers

Like the passengers on the *Titanic,* it's easy for us to get lulled into comfort and miss some critical warning signs of life's journey. And like Jeremy, it's easy to overestimate our strength against seductive temptations. We need to be constantly on the lookout for hidden dangers. And we need to look to God as our authority. The story of Micaiah in 1 Kings 22 is a good example.

As the story unfolds, the king of Judah (the southern kingdom) asks King Jehoshaphat of Israel (the northern kingdom) to join forces with him in reclaiming some land an enemy had taken. So the king of Israel brought together his four hundred prophets and asked them if he should go to war. Because they were on the king's payroll, they had all learned to say exactly what the king wanted to hear. With one voice they all affirmed his plan.

But Jehoshaphat was smart enough not to be fooled by his own "yes men."

"Is there not a prophet of the Lord here whom we can inquire of?" he asked King Ahab.

There was only one man Ahab could think of, but it was someone he couldn't stand—Micaiah. Why? Because Micaiah always told the truth based on the authority of God's Word to him, not what Ahab wanted to hear. Ahab hoped to keep Micaiah under wraps, so he wouldn't tell it like it was. But Jehoshaphat insisted.

Ahab sent his chief of priests, Zedekiah, to fetch Micaiah— but also to warn him. Zedekiah told Micaiah that the king's prophets had predicted success and, if he knew what was good for him, Micaiah would do the same. Without hesitation, Micaiah simply said he would speak what the Lord told him to say.

Arriving at the scene of two kings and four hundred prophets, all of whom had given their go-ahead for rushing headlong into battle, Micaiah sized up the picture quickly. When he was asked what the kings should do, he replied sarcastically, "Oh sure, go ahead. I'm just confident (ha, ha) that God will give you success." Jehoshaphat would have none of that. He knew that Micaiah wasn't leveling, and he pushed for a straight answer. So Micaiah stood on conviction and warned that, if they went to battle, they would be scattered like the sheep in the hills. He predicted that, if Ahab went into battle, he wouldn't return alive. Guess what happened. The leader of the false prophets stepped forward and slugged Micaiah for not going along with the crowd!

The kings did go to battle and, as Micaiah predicted, Ahab was killed. So what are the lessons we can take from this remarkable event in history? Can we count on what the experts say? How about people in authority? Is the majority usually right? Can we trust our feelings?

The Experts Aren't Always Right

Have you ever stopped to think how often those who are called experts aren't very expert in their outcomes? Sometimes people characterized as having the greatest insight just don't have a clue. Consider these examples:

- Coaches said Michael Jordan should be cut from the ninth-grade basketball team because he didn't have talent.
- Thomas Edison's teachers said he was too stupid to learn anything.
- Walt Disney was fired by a newspaper editor who thought he lacked creative ideas.
- When a fiery redhead auditioned for a role on a television show, the producer watched her, then replied, "Get a job, any job . . . because you'll never be an actress." The young woman's name was Lucille Ball.
- When a lanky aspiring actor read for a screen role, the director said, "Your Adam's apple is too big. You're too skinny. And you're way too monotone. You'll never make it in this business." The aspiring actor happened to be Clint Eastwood.

Some experts do something so long and so well they start taking for granted that everything will always go right, so they let down their guard for just a moment, confident they're unsinkable. Their mantra seems to be, "I know what I'm doing. I'm an expert!"

This reminds me of Roy Horn of Siegfried and Roy, the amazing illusionist duo who have been a centerpiece of Las Vegas shows for years at the Mirage. Hundreds of thousands of tourists have sat mesmerized by their illusions that rival David Copperfield—only with breathtaking wild animals like white Siberian tigers. Roy called them his pets. Then one night in October of 2003, a tiger turned on Roy and almost ripped his throat out. The audience didn't realize what was happening for several horrifying moments. Stagehands used fire extinguishers to distract the tiger and rescue the illusionist—an expert in animal behavior. No one saw the attack coming.

People in positions of authority aren't always right, either.

When Joycelyn Elders was surgeon general for the United States under President Clinton, two of her ideas were to

1. Legalize drugs as a way of reducing crime.
2. Instruct girls to carry condoms in their purses when they go on dates. Dr. Elders said, "We taught [teens] what to do in the front seat [of the car]. . . . Now it's time to teach them what to do in the back seat."[7]

By the way, her son was convicted of illegal drug use and sentenced for cocaine trafficking. And science has proven that condoms don't prevent certain sexually transmitted diseases!

Or how about the prolific writer who many of us heard about in our literature classes—Ernest Hemingway? He said, "Immorality is (only) what you feel bad after." Hemingway was known for his affairs with women, his drinking and partying, and his live-it-to-the-max lifestyle. I wonder if that's why he put a shotgun in his mouth and pulled the trigger?

Or how about our Supreme Court system that saw fit on January 22, 1973, to pass *Roe v. Wade,* which legalized abortion on demand? The medical community began to call abortion *post-contraceptive fertility control.* Suddenly the fetus was no longer talked about as a child, a baby, or an individual, but simply as an object of fertility control. Now, more than 44 million abortions later, we're still reaping tragic results from a ruling to establish that "legal personhood does not exist prenatally . . ." And now in our society a baby is aborted every thirty seconds!

Instead, the experts tell us . . .

- A woman isn't accountable to anyone but herself when it comes to her body! My question: What about the baby's body, let alone the baby's life?
- Smart people are pro-choice! My question: Is that the same as pro-death?
- Don't worry about abortion—it's safe! My question: Safe for whom? It's definitely not safe for the baby!

No, the experts aren't always right.

The Majority Isn't Always Right

Another false claim is that the majority is always right. Oh yeah? I'll give you some examples to contradict that.

President Abraham Lincoln was deeply committed to freeing slaves and abolishing slavery. He proposed the Emancipation Proclamation but decided to share his plan first with those he trusted the most, his Cabinet. They voted seven nays and two ayes. Stunned by the negative majority, Lincoln thought for a moment, then said, "Well, we voted, and it looks like the ayes have it!" History has shown that the majority was anything but right!

The majority opinion often misses the mark. A growing majority of people in today's culture say, "If you want to live together, great, it's nobody else's business!" But statistics prove . . .

- Among people who live together before marriage, there's a 50 percent *higher* rate of divorce than married couples who did not live together first.
- Cohabitation increases young people's acceptance of divorce. The longer people have lived together unmarried, the less enthusiastic they are about a lifelong commitment.
- Cohabiting couples report lower levels of happiness, lower levels of sexual faithfulness and sexual satisfaction, and poorer relationships with their parents than do married couples.
- Unmarried individuals who live together are three times more likely to be depressed than married persons.
- Women in cohabiting relationships are more likely than married women to suffer physical or sexual abuse.

So much for the majority of our television shows and movies, which glamorize and idealize sex before marriage. There are even lines of clothes that do the same. Do you shop at a store that so many students flock to—Abercrombie & Fitch? Oh, I understand, you like the *clothes!* But have you ever taken time to look beyond the clothes? The Abercrombie & Fitch catalog is little more than a pornographic magazine. In the summer 2003 edition its pages were filled with photographs of nude teenagers embracing and rolling around on the beach, in the water and in the grass. You'd expect those photos in a porn magazine but not in a clothing magazine whose main audience is teenagers. So you may be part of a huge group who like the clothes, but do you realize what your money is going to support?

By the way, my encouragement to you, if you're serious about your relationship to Christ and standing for what He said is important, is to *stand firm* and not buy anything from Abercrombie & Fitch in the future. The question for all of us comes down to: *Do our beliefs have enough strength in our lives to impact our actions?*

Feelings Aren't Always Right

I live in Atlanta, and sometimes the traffic is horrendous! It can switch from a massive five-mile parking lot to a NASCAR racetrack in a matter of seconds. Cars constantly zip around you, pushing you out of your lane. Last week a car whipped in front of me, almost driving me into the car to my left. Fighting to regain control of my vehicle, I finally righted myself in the center of the lane and pulled up behind the nut who had rudely cut me off. On his back bumper was a sticker that said, "*IF IT FEELS GOOD, DO IT.*"

Suddenly—I don't know where this came from—I had this creeping urge to put the pedal to the metal and ram him from the back! I could just see the outcome as our cars careened off the road and finally came to a rest. In my mind I could see him storming out of his car and pounding the turf back to me and screaming, "What did you do *that* for?" And I could picture myself quietly sitting there, smiling and saying, "I was just doing what you told me to do—if it feels good, do it. *And it felt great!*" I don't think the police would buy my explanation. And neither would my insurance company! Feelings just aren't a good judge for making sound decisions.

Here's another example.

It was a perfect day. A perfect plan. A perfect couple. As the charismatic and handsome couple launched out for their day, everything seemed ideal. The destination—a family wedding they'd looked forward to with great anticipation. They traveled by private plane, talking and laughing about their upcoming weekend of celebration with family and friends. They discussed the hopes they had for the soon-to-be newlyweds. And their world seemed like its own Camelot, perfect in every way.

Until something horrible happened. The husband began anxiously to search the horizon. The sky was getting dark. He was a pilot, but he hadn't earned his instrument rating. Now he could only fly on his feelings, and they were telling him he was headed in the right direction. But a problem called vertigo set in. He became disoriented. As night engulfed the plane he became more dependent on his feelings because he was only qualified to fly visually.

In the hazy evening sky, as the plane turned right and began to climb, the husband suffered spatial disorientation. The plane briefly leveled before turning right and making a fatally fast descent, reaching speeds that topped ten times what was considered normal for the aircraft. And then it crashed into the ocean, and everything was silent.

John F. Kennedy Jr. and his beautiful wife, Caroline Bessette Kennedy, perished in their small plane on July 16, 1999. But almost to the point of the crash, Kennedy probably felt he had his Cessna 182 under control, another tragic example of dependence on feelings which are rarely trustworthy!

But . . . God Is Never Wrong!

To me, one of the Bible's most amazing chapters is Isaiah 45. If you turn there and read through it you'll discover that four separate times God says these words, *"I am the LORD God, and there is no other."* I find that when God repeats something to me, He's trying to get a message across. Sometimes I'm a little bit slow on the uptake, so He wants to make sure I don't miss it.

In between those four statements we discover why there's only one God, and none other. Throughout the chapter, God talks about all that He has created and all that He controls. He refers to the amazing works of His hands. And then in Isaiah 46:10 He says, "My plan will take place, and I will do all My will."

By following God we seem to be swimming upstream against the tide of society that tries to convince us the majority is always right, experts know best, and feelings can be trusted. But, if we go with the flow of society, we'll sink like the *Titanic*. God always has your best interests at heart, and He always knows what's right for your life. He reminds us of this truth in these verses you should always remember:

- **God's priority for your life**—"I have loved you with an everlasting love; therefore, I have continued to extend faithful love to you" (Jeremiah 31:3).
- **God's plan for your life**—"'I know the plans that I have for you,' declares the LORD, 'plans to prosper you and not to harm you, plans to give you hope and a future. Then you will call upon me and come and pray to me, and I will listen to you. You will seek me and find me when you seek me with all your heart'" (Jeremiah 29:11–13 NIV).
- **God's provision for your life**—"And my God will supply all your needs according to His riches in glory in Christ Jesus" (Philippians 4:19).
- **God's protection for your life**—"The one who lives under the protection of the Most High dwells in the shadow of the Almighty. I will say to the LORD, 'My refuge and my fortress, my God, in whom I trust'" (Psalm 91:1–2).

Charting Your Own Course

ANDY

I f the experts knew all they claim to know, I would never have become a big league ballplayer. In 1990 the Yankees drafted me out of high school in the twenty-second round of the amateur draft. Getting drafted was great. It meant some scout thought I could pitch, but getting drafted that low meant no one expected me to do much more than labor in the minor leagues. To put my position in perspective you need to understand the NFL only has six rounds in their draft, and the NBA has two. Hundreds of other guys were picked before me, and only 1 or 2 percent of them would ever make it to the majors. Needless to say, I wasn't exactly the hot prospect of the 1990 draft.

Rather than sign with the Yankees I enrolled at San Jacinto Junior College where my coach, Wayne Graham, impressed on me the importance of getting stronger and working my body into great shape. The pro scouts didn't think I could throw hard enough to make it to the big leagues, so I started working to improve my velocity. After one year of college ball I signed with New York where I surprised everyone by throwing a lot harder than anyone expected. They sent me to their rookie league team in Tampa, and I started my climb through their minor league system. But moving up to Double A or Triple A ball wasn't my goal. So I kept working and trying to improve even though I knew the odds were against me.

I can count on one hand the number of guys I played with in the minors who made it to the majors. If the experts had been right about me I wouldn't have made it either. But my goal has never been to live down to other people's expectations. I want to become the best pitcher in baseball. That's my goal. I don't know if I can be, but that's what I'm shooting for. Sure, I hear the voices telling me I can't. In my second year in the majors I had doctors tell me my elbow wasn't going to last through the season. They told me my ligaments were tearing and I would have to have radical surgery soon. I have to tell you, for a twenty-three-year-old kid that was scary to hear, especially after just making the Yankees the year before. But obviously the doctors were wrong. I was bound and determined if something was wrong in my elbow, I would work on it and make it stronger so it would hold up for me. And it has.

That's why I'm telling you that you don't have to live down to other people's expectations. Let's be honest; the world doesn't expect a lot out of us as guys. Everyone pretty much expects us to cuss and to cheat and to be obsessed with sex. They say looking at pornography or undressing girls with your eyes are just part of being a normal male. But they are wrong. The so-called experts aren't the ones who tell you what you must be. God has that job and He says, "For I am the LORD your God, so you must consecrate yourselves and be holy because I am holy" (Leviticus 11:44). Some people would say that is impossible, but the Bible says, "I can do all things through Christ who strengthens me" (Philippians 4:13 NKJV).

So break out of the mold. Be what God made you to be. Commit yourself to a life of integrity and purity. I'm not going to lie to you and tell you it will be easy. I've been where you are now. I know the kinds of pressures you feel because I felt them myself. But just because this commitment is difficult to keep doesn't mean you should give up. No goal worth reaching comes easily. Why would the goal of purity be any different?

When Others Give Up on You

Living out your commitment to purity can also seem more difficult when the people around you appear to give up on you. It happens. You mess up or make a bad decision and people automatically assume the worst. Sometimes they do this even when you don't mess up yourself. One of your friends gets into trouble and suddenly people assume you are no different than him. It's not just guilt by association. People you look up to, people you trust, stop trusting you. They've given up on you and nothing you say makes any difference. The temptation is to go ahead and throw away your commitment. If people assume the worst about you, why disappoint them?

Remember: just because people give up on you, that doesn't mean you should give up on yourself.

One of the hardest times I've had in my baseball career came in the middle of the 1999 season. I had a lot of success over my first few years in the big leagues. In four seasons I compiled a record of sixty-seven wins and thirty-five losses. In 1996 I won twenty-one games and finished second in the American League Cy Young race. I followed that up with an eighteen-win season in '97 with an earned run average of less than three. But I struggled at the start of the '99 season. At one point I'd only won five games and lost eight. The critics started saying I'd thrown too many cut fastballs and my arm was wearing down. Some of the higher-ups in the Yankee organization were thinking the league had figured me out and that my best days were behind me.

That wasn't the worst of it. My contract was up for renewal at the end of the season. Based on the success I'd had early in my career I was set to get a really big contract. But now the team wasn't so sure they should resign me. That's when the rumors started. The team started talking about trading me in the middle of the season to try to get something for me while they still could. Every time I turned around I heard another rumor of how the Yankees were about to trade me to the Philadelphia Phillies. It appeared the organization had thrown in the towel on me. They'd given up. They now expected me to fail.

The stress took its toll. My wife could hardly sleep because of the constant uncertainty. A trade to Philadelphia wouldn't affect only me. The lives of everyone in our family would be touched by it. Our oldest son was in school, and a trade meant changing schools and friends for him. Then we would have to sell our house and find a place in Philly, all this while I adjusted to a new team and a new league.

The rumors reached a level where it sounded like a trade was a done deal. But rather than let them get to me, I moved closer to the Lord. I knew my life and the lives of my family were in His hands. So rather than worry about things over which I had no control, I trusted God to work things out His way. He gave me a great peace. I knew I couldn't do anything except keep working. And that's what I did. I went out to the bull pen and tried to figure out what was wrong. In the end the Yankees didn't trade me. Joe Torre stuck his neck out for me and convinced the team not to get rid of me. Mel Stottlemyre worked with me and we were able to turn my season around. I finished with a record of fourteen and eleven, and the team gave me a four-year contract in the off-season.

Here's my point: If I'd given up on myself when the team did, my season and possibly my career would have been over. But I trusted in the Lord and did everything I needed to do to prove the critics wrong. That's what you need to do. No one else may believe you are serious about your commitment to purity. But it doesn't matter what they may think. Don't give up on yourself or on God. You can do this, even if no one believes you can.

The Wrong Choice Feels Right

You can keep your commitment to purity, but it won't be easy. At times the biggest hurdle you will face will be yourself. You won't always want to say no to temptation because the thought of giving in will sound pretty good. In those moments you have to choose to follow Christ, not your feelings. We have to do what we know is right, not what feels right. Every day you and I face decisions that either lift us up and make us more like Jesus or drag us further from Him. The girls you date, the group you hang out with, the movies you watch, and the music you listen to will all either raise you up or pull you down. You can't just make these decisions on what feels right or what you most want to do. God has to have the final say.

I thought I would enjoy being a free agent at the end of the 2003 season, but it didn't take long for it to turn into a headache. In my heart I couldn't imagine playing for anyone but New York. I'd spent my entire career with the team. I didn't just play for the Yankees; I was a Yankee. But that wasn't the only reason I couldn't imagine leaving New York. If I stayed there, I could possibly become the winningest pitcher in Yankee history and break a bunch of other records as well. After nine seasons I found myself within reach of guys I thought of as legends, guys with statues in monument park in Yankee Stadium. How could I walk away from that?

But where I played baseball wasn't really my decision. All my personal feelings didn't matter. What did matter was God's will. I needed to know what He wanted me to do. As the offers started coming in from other teams, hearing God's voice got harder. The Boston Red Sox blew everyone else away by opening the bidding with an offer of $54 million over four seasons. But I knew I would never sign with the Yankees' biggest rival. I couldn't do that to my teammates in New York. Yet that didn't mean God wanted me to re-sign with the Yankees. My wife and I prayed and prayed over the decision, and we asked our church family and friends across the country to pray for us.

As we prayed, God started closing doors in New York and opening doors for me to sign with the team closest to my home, the Houston Astros. Even though I sensed God leading us in this direction, it was still hard for me to let go of the Yankees. I could've ignored God and done what I wanted, but anytime you are out of God's will you are asking for trouble. If you don't follow His plan, sooner or later your rope will break and you will find yourself on your knees asking Him, "Why did I go in this direction?" In the end I left New York and signed with the Astros. I ended up signing for a lot less money than I could have made somewhere else, but that wasn't the issue.

If you go with your head and just look at what the world thinks is important, you will be led one way. And if you allow your feelings and desires to lead you, you will go another way. But for those of us who claim Jesus as our Savior, only one thing matters, and that's being where God wants us to be, doing what pleases Him.

Adjusting to Whatever the Enemy Throws at Us

Living a life of purity pleases God, but it makes Satan angry. He wants to do anything he can to trip you up and make you fall. The longer you keep your commitment to purity, the madder he gets. But he doesn't give up. He'll constantly change his strategy to try to find a weakness in your life he can exploit. If one approach doesn't work, he quickly tries something else. Because the enemy's strategy is constantly evolving, the course we chart toward a life that pleases God must evolve as well. We need to be flexible so that we can deal with whatever he throws at us.

I have to do this as a ballplayer. The average player comes up and plays maybe four or five years. If you are going to last longer you have to continue to elevate your game and let it evolve. There are the rare exceptions. Roger Clemens threw a ninety-five-mile-per-hour fastball and a split-fingered fastball throughout his career. When you can throw as hard as he can, you get guys out on sheer power. But I'm not a power pitcher. I have to rely on location, which means being able to throw the ball where the batter doesn't expect it to be.

When I first came up I had a real good changeup, a good curve, and a pretty good fastball. That was all. Those pitches might have been enough when I was a rookie, but it wouldn't take long for hitters to figure me out.

In 1996 I learned to throw the cut fastball and I stopped throwing changeups. That season guys would come up to bat against me, and they would sit back and wait for me to throw the change. Once they stopped looking for the change and started looking for some other pitch, I changed my approach again. In fact, in my first nine seasons in the big leagues I completely remade myself as a pitcher five times.

When I moved from the American League to the National I faced another challenge. Pitchers don't bat in the AL because of the designated hitter rule, but they do in the NL. To prepare myself for the change, I added daily batting practice to my off-season workout routine, along with extra cardiovascular conditioning for base running. New challenges mean new adjustments if I am going to continue to be successful as a pitcher.

I not only have to make adjustments from year to year; I also have to change from game to game. When I warm up before a start, I never really know which pitches are going to work that night. I may not be able to throw my two-seamer down and away to a right-handed hitter. That means it's going to be a tough night. I will have to throw a lot more curveballs to keep guys off balance and throw in some changeups. Other nights my fastball is jumping and I'll go with that. I also have to adjust to what the other team is looking for and what they are hitting that night. If I try to approach every start the exact same way, I'll get lit up.

I have to make constant adjustments, and all I face is another baseball team. The stakes are much higher in your quest to live a life that pleases God. What worked yesterday may not work today. That's why you have to stay flexible in your approach and fresh in your relationship with God. This commitment is too important to coast through. The course you set needs to draw you closer to God. Together, you can overcome anything.

Study Questions

- Read 1 Kings 18:16–39 and pay close attention to the actions of the crowd. Whose side were they on, Elijah's or the prophets of Baal? Give yourself a bonus point if you said neither. They were for whomever seemed to be winning at the moment. What does this tell you about the value of majority opinions? How hard is it for you to go against the majority and chart your own course? When have you felt the pressure to conform to the crowd? Did the pressure come mostly from other people or from within yourself? Did you give in? Why or why not? What do you need if you are going to consistently walk with Christ instead of going along with everyone else?

- Living a life of purity would be much easier if doing the wrong thing resulted in instant pain rather than pleasure. Have you experienced the battle between what feels right and what you know to be right? Tell me about it. Which did you choose? Why? What was the right choice? What difference would a different decision have made?

- Has someone you loved or respected ever given up on you? What impact did this have on the subsequent choices you made?

- How are the temptations you face today different than those you faced ten years ago (if you can remember that far back)? Five years ago? Look ahead. A day is coming when you will move out of your parents' house and be on your own. How will your commitment to purity be tested then? What kind of adjustments do you need to make today to be ready?

Sometimes You Have to Take a Stand

CHAPTER SEVEN

Isn't Purity Just for Wimps?

BOB

Charles Blondin dreamed of being an acrobat. From the age of six, he was determined to walk on a tightrope. And at an early age, his dream became reality. He became known as the "Little Wonder." His daring exploits and hazardous feats boggled the minds of observers who gasped and held their breath as they watched him.

But nothing took their breath away like his exhibitions in 1859 and 1860 when he stretched a tightrope 1,100 feet across Niagara Falls, towering 160 feet above the raging waters. Then he grabbed his balance pole and, to the horror and amazement of thousands, took off across the rain-slicked cable to be the first man to transverse the falls on a tightrope. But he wasn't finished. He walked across the falls blindfolded, with a man on his back, riding a bicycle, and even carrying a small stove to the middle of the rope where he knelt down, cooked an omelet, and lowered it to the tourist boat far below for a spectator to eat!

Then he took a wheelbarrow and pushed it across. After loading it up with rocks, he pushed it across again, and the crowd went wild! When the cheering died down, he asked if those watching believed he could put a man from the crowd in the wheelbarrow and push him across without falling into the water. Again, the crowd cheered at the top of their voices.

Suddenly, Blondin pointed to a man standing in the front and said, "Then get in!" That man and every one near the front scrambled away. No one would volunteer. Everybody agreed Blondin could do it, *until* he asked one of them to turn his belief into conviction and climb in the wheelbarrow to prove it.

That happens a lot in life. Anyone can say he believes this or that because, frankly, *believing* is easy. But when it comes to the conviction of *acting* on the belief . . . that's a different story!

Conviction Is More than Belief

Nobody demonstrates this better than Daniel in the Old Testament. Daniel was a young man growing up with great promise in the land of Judah when Nebuchadnezzar became king of Babylon. In the fall of 605 BC, Nebuchadnezzar and the Babylonian army attacked Judah and surrounded the capitol, Jerusalem. When the city fell, they captured the most handsome and intelligent guys and the most gifted and beautiful girls and took them away to Babylon.

And that included Daniel. He was probably a teen when the Babylonian army ripped him from his home and dragged him off to Babylonia as a slave. They also took three of his friends: Shadrach, Meshach, and Abednego. All four had been raised to believe in the living God and His desire for them to have a personal relationship with Him. Even their names reflected their parents' commitment to follow God. Daniel's name in his native Hebrew language meant, "God is my judge." Shadrach's name meant, "The Lord shows grace." Meshach's name asked, "Who is like God?" And Abednego's name declared, "The Lord helps."

But now, suddenly, they found themselves captives in a strange land. Their captors didn't just make them slaves. They tried to force Daniel and his friends to adapt to their culture. The Babylonians changed their Hebrew names to Babylonian names in an effort to strip away their identities and their loyalty to God. Then they shoved a new way of seeing the world down their throats by re-educating them in the Babylonian way. Daniel and his friends might have wondered: *Where is God? If He helps, then how about some help right now? And if He's so powerful, then why can't He get us out of here?*

The worst part was this: Their captors insisted they eat food forbidden by God. Though Scripture doesn't declare it specifically, it's likely the food they were given had been sacrificed to idols. Yet these young men had been raised to believe there's only one God, and they should serve Him alone. Eating any food that had been offered to false gods was out-of-bounds, for that simple act would symbolize that they believed the false gods were real. These teens found themselves at the crossroads of decision—what would they do?

It was Daniel who first stepped up and took action. According to Daniel 1:8 "he resolved not to defile himself with the royal food and wine" (NIV). The word *resolved* indicates strong conviction to a course of action. His words went beyond mere belief in God to convictions that forced him *to do what's right no matter what!* Conviction is always grounded in belief that leads to action based on values we hold to be critically important and right—*regardless* of circumstances, personal desires, and peer pressure.

Notice how Daniel handled himself in this difficult situation. When you read the story in Daniel 1 you find he didn't belligerently refuse to obey the king. He didn't lash out in anger or make a scene. Instead, he asked for permission not to defile himself with the king's food, and he offered a creative alternative. He would eat a diet of vegetables for ten days and then allow himself to be examined to see if he was doing just as well as those who ate the food that was sacrificed to idols.

There's an important lesson here about conviction. I've heard Josh McDowell so often say, "When you are standing on conviction, aggressively live in love, and humbly stand for the truth." Daniel modeled this perfectly. He found a way to stand on his conviction to follow God's will in the midst of a culture pushing him to do the convenient thing, which was to follow the king's orders and acknowledge the false gods.

Convictions worth standing on must be based on absolute truth. And absolute truth means it's a truth applicable *for all people, at all times, and in all places.* The man with conviction—who takes action based on his belief—doesn't change because of circumstances. He stands firm *no matter what.*

Are there exceptions? Let's fast-forward about twenty-five hundred years from Daniel to a high school senior named Chad. He made a pledge to live a pure life—no lying, cheating, or stealing, no sex before marriage, that sort of thing. But he's with his buddies and somebody suggests they pop in a porn DVD. Chad and the guys are in the basement and the folks are out 'til midnight. He rationalizes, *It's only looking, not doing.* Or Chad's girlfriend keeps saying oral sex isn't *real* sex, so he thinks, *Well, tonight is prom night, so maybe just this one time.* Is Chad thinking like a man of conviction? Is Chad's behavior resisting his pressure from others? Is Chad standing firm, *no matter what?*

How would Daniel handle those scenes? Would he impose his convictions on his friends in the basement? Sure, it would be nice if he modeled what he claimed to believe—and they followed his lead. But, even if they didn't, he could remove himself from the situation. If "I wanna go back to ESPN" doesn't cut it with Chad's friends, he could say, "That's not for me, guys. I'm outta here." He could tell his girlfriend that talking about oral sex isn't helping them stay pure, and if she doesn't cut it out he will have to break it off with her.

Would he be wimping out? No, he'd be acting like a man of conviction.

According to Josh McDowell, "A conviction goes beyond having a personal preference about something. It goes deeper than a subjective opinion. Having convictions is being so thoroughly convinced that something is absolutely true that you take a stand for it regardless of the consequences. That's the kind of belief in God and His Word our kids need."[8]

Daniel was not a New Testament Christian because he lived in Old Testament times, but he understood the principle that would be stated later in 2 Corinthians 5:9 where Paul said, "We make it our aim to be pleasing to Him." That attitude is what drove Daniel's conviction. He wanted his whole life to please God. He wasn't intent on alienating anybody but on serving the One who had created him.

That's exactly what Paul meant about the ultimate proof of worshipping God in Romans 12:1–2: "Therefore, brothers, by the mercies of God, I urge you to present your bodies as a living sacrifice, holy and pleasing to God; this is your spiritual worship. Do not be conformed to this age, but be transformed by the renewing of your mind, so that you may discern what is the good, pleasing, and perfect will of God."

Even before Paul challenged the believers in Rome with these words, Daniel was finding out just how good, trustworthy, and true God's will is when you don't allow yourself to be pressed into the mold of the culture around you. Anybody can go with the flow. In fact, wimps can do that! But it takes a person of maturity, strength of character, depth of conviction, and authentic leadership to stand pure and undefiled, like Daniel.

Living by Conviction Has Impact on Others

Remember Daniel's resolve to deny himself the food the Babylonians were trying to force on him? After ten days he looked even healthier and better nourished than all the others who had eaten royal food. Once he passed the test, all the rich food was carted away, and Daniel and his friends were allowed to follow their convictions. In response to their obedience, God gave Daniel and his three friends knowledge in all of their studies (bet you could use some of that!). They became leaders appointed by the king. In fact, the king found no one else equal to these four. "In every matter of wisdom and understanding that the king consulted them about, he found them *10 times better* than all the diviner-priests and mediums in his entire kingdom" (Daniel 1:20, emphasis added).

When our actions demonstrate that not only do we believe what God says but are willing to act on it, God becomes responsible for the results. But beware, our obedience doesn't always mean a smooth or easy road.

As time went on, Nebuchadnezzar lost track of the God whom Daniel so faithfully served. In fact, one day Nebuchadnezzar decided he was a god. As a result, he made a ninety-feet-high and nine-feet-wide statue of gold of himself and set it out for all people to worship. He announced that as soon as the people heard the music of celebration they were to fall down and worship this golden statue. And the kicker was, whoever did not fall down and worship it would be immediately thrown into a blazing furnace.

Shadrach, Meshach, and Abednego had noticed years earlier how Daniel had stood so firmly on his convictions regardless of the consequences. It's an amazing thing when that happens. When someone has the courage to stand on convictions of absolute truth according to the guidelines God has given for maximum living, it always affects people around them. And Shadrach, Meshach, and Abednego were no exceptions.

So now it was their turn! And they had a couple of options. They could *compromise* their faith, or they could *conceal* it. And why not compromise? If ever there was a situation where it must have "felt right" to compromise, this was it. The alternative was to be roasted like a chicken on a rotisserie. Think of the rationalizations and excuses they could have come up with to justify compromising their convictions! Try these on for size . . .

- We will bow down but not actually worship the idol in our hearts!
- The king has absolute power, and we have to do what he says. God will understand!
- We won't actually become idol worshippers, but appearing to worship the idol this one time won't hurt!
- This is a foreign land, so God will overlook this!
- This won't be half as bad as some of the things other people do!
- This won't hurt anybody!
- If we get killed, then God will have no one in the positions we now hold!
- We can handle this! It won't make us stumble!

Any of the excuses sound familiar? These guys chose not to use ANY of them! No compromise for them.

The other option they had was to conceal their faith. They might have been thinking, *If we let everybody see our faith, we won't fit in. If we just keep quiet, things will cool off, and we can make a difference later! Better to wait for a more convenient time to do this witnessing and living by faith stuff.*

But they didn't hide their confidence in the Lord. Instead, bolstered by what they had witnessed in Daniel's faith, they made a pact to stand their ground with conviction. When they heard the music, they refused to fall down and worship the idol. They only had one Person to worship, and His name was Jehovah God.

Today we don't have statues ninety feet high and nine feet wide made of gold, but we still have idols. Anthropologists tell us that an idol is anything that's so sacred to us that it defines our self-worth and becomes the controlling center of our lives. It becomes the last thing we want to let go of.[9] Is there anything, or anyone, in your life that's providing you with your sense of self-worth? Or how about something that's the last thing you'd ever want to let go of? If so, does it strangely remind you of a big, golden statue in a place called Babylon?

When Shadrach, Meshach, and Abednego refused to fall down and worship, the king had to follow through with his threat. He commanded that they be gathered up and thrown into a fiery furnace. Were these guys wimps? You decide when you read what they said just before they were cast into the fire: "Nebuchadnezzar, we don't need to give you an answer to this question. If the God we serve exists, then He can rescue us from the furnace of blazing fire, and He can rescue us from the power of you, the king. *But even if He does not* rescue us, we want you as king to know that we will not serve your gods or worship the gold statue you set up" (Daniel 3:16–18, emphasis added).

Can you say that? Can you say that God is able to see you through when you have to stand by conviction, but even if He chooses not to, you're still willing to stand firm? That's what a man of conviction says.

The rest of the story gets even better. They were thrown into the furnace. It was so hot that it killed the people who threw them in, but the flames didn't touch Shadrach, Meshach, or Abednego. They walked around in the fire like they were going for a stroll through their old neighborhood. Yet when the king looked in later he didn't see three people, he saw four. He said the fourth looked like "the Son of God" (Daniel 3:25 NKJV). Jesus had come to the rescue!

And when the three were delivered out of the furnace, what happened to the One who had protected them? Could it be that He stayed in there because He knew sooner or later you and I would need to be delivered? He's still waiting to see you and me through when we stand firmly on conviction, even when it gets hot!

Living by Conviction Has Long-Term Impact

We can't leave this chapter without remembering that when you start living by conviction early in life, it's a habit that keeps on keeping on. It did for Daniel. We saw what he did when he was your age, but the story doesn't stop there. Many years later, when Daniel was at least eighty years of age, another king took power. Daniel was still living by conviction, and he had proven himself to be such a man of integrity that the new king planned to put Daniel in a key position to rule over the whole kingdom.

An amazing thing about success is this: when you're blessed with it, sometimes those around you are angry with you because of it. Their jealously leads them to look for ways to hold you back or tear you down so they can look better. The same thing happened to Daniel.

His coworkers decided to play to the king's ego and entice him to pronounce an edict saying that during the next thirty days, anybody caught praying to any god or man except the king would be thrown in the lions' den. In an ego-saturated moment, the king signed the law. And when Daniel refused to stop praying three times a day to the God who had been so faithful to him throughout the years, the king had no choice but to follow his own order. Heartbroken, he commanded that Daniel be thrown in the den with the lions knowing that he would grieve the loss of his advisor, counselor, and friend. Surely the next morning his body would be found in the den, torn and shredded by the savage beasts.

Imagine how stunned the king was the next day when the guards found Daniel safe and secure and testifying that God had protected him through the night. The king was so overjoyed that he ordered those who falsely accused Daniel to be thrown into the lions' den instead. He then commanded that all of the kingdom should fear and reverence the God of Daniel who had proved Himself so mightily.

You just can't get away from it. Living by conviction pays off—BIG TIME!

Daniel honored God, and God, in turn, honored Daniel. Don't you want to get in on some of that action?

Standing Up by Standing Out

ANDY

When you decide to honor God in every part of your life, you will be different. You can't help it. Light and darkness can never be the same. The way you talk, the way you act, the attitudes you have about yourself and other people, everything you do shows whether God is really in your heart. And when He is, you will be a part of the odd crowd.

But that doesn't mean you have to make a big show out of how different you are. Sometimes we read stories of people like Daniel and Shadrach, Meshach, and Abednego and we think we have to make big public stands for God to make a difference. If that were true I would be in trouble. I'm not real vocal. I don't like going around ruffling people's feathers. And I've never been one to make a big show about anything. That doesn't mean I'm ashamed of Christ or that I will compromise my convictions to keep from offending people. I stand up when I need to, but sometimes taking a big, public stand like Shadrach, Meshach, and Abednego is a lot easier than being consistent in our day-to-day walk with Christ.

And our day-to-day consistency is the real test of our convictions. Every day you and I face choices. The Holy Spirit who lives inside of us along with our consciences push us one direction. Satan and our flesh push us another. You and I have to decide which one we will listen to. As we continue to make the right choices, it becomes easier to do the right thing when temptation comes. It is sort of like my workout routine. If I miss a workout here and a workout there, it then becomes easier and easier to miss workouts. In the same way, if we don't make daily right choices, it gets easier and easier to make wrong choices. The next thing you know you aren't reading your Bible anymore and you aren't praying anymore and you aren't fellowshipping with other Christians anymore. Then it becomes that much easier to make choices you will regret the rest of your life. Satan will have you right where he wants you. It is just that easy. You have to be consistent. That's the first stand you have to take for Christ.

Consistency On and Off the Field

Living consistently for Christ is like pitching. It is all about control. Success as a pitcher comes from being able to control your body and your emotions. God has enabled me to carry myself the same way no matter what is happening with baseball. I know when I take the pitcher's mound I have a responsibility to always uphold my testimony. That's why I've been successful in the big leagues. Whether I'm struggling or pitching better than ever, I want to be the same person. It's not easy. Sometimes my emotions come out and I may punch something in the dugout, but I do my best to keep that from happening. There is no doubt I am at my best when I am focused and concentrating on trying to get hitters out and not thinking about anything else.

Keeping my emotions in check and doing my best to live my testimony on the field doesn't diminish my competitive fire. Far from it. I hate to lose, especially in a big game. And few games were bigger than Game 6 of the 2003 World Series. We were down three games to two to the Florida Marlins and had to win to stay alive. Their ace, Josh Beckett, started the game and looked untouchable. I got the start for the Yankees, my second of the series. In Game 2 I shut down the Marlins and only gave up one unearned run in eight and two-thirds innings.

Josh and I traded zeroes on the scoreboard through the first four innings of Game 6. We'd both given up a handful of hits and both teams had chances to score, but Josh and I both were able to get key outs to keep the game scoreless.

In the top of the fifth inning I got two quick outs on the Florida Marlins after striking out their first baseman Derrek Lee and getting right fielder Juan Encarnacion to ground out. But then Alex Gonzalez and Juan Pierre hit back-to-back singles to center field, and I was looking at the possibility of this inning getting away from me. As their second baseman, Luis Castillo, came up to bat, I knew I wanted to shut them down and get this guy out. My first pitch to him was a called strike, and he swung and missed the next for strike two. As a pitcher, this is where I wanted to get this guy. But he kept battling and fouled off a couple of pitches and laid off a couple more. Then I threw a ball that was on the outside corner and he just sort of slapped it the other way. Our right fielder, Karim Garcia, fielded the weak hit on one hop and threw it to home as Gonzalez tried to score from second. The play was close, but our catcher, Jorge Posada, couldn't make the tag and the run scored.

At that moment I was probably as mad as I have ever been in a game. I knew Josh was throwing a great game for Florida, and it was going to be tough to score a run on him. And to tell you the truth, I knew I was good that night and I didn't think they were going to score a run against me. Then I went and gave up that run with two outs in the inning, and I was mad. I was furious. But I didn't show it. I had to stay in control and keep my focus on getting the next hitter. If I lost it out on the mound, I might easily give up several more runs. You can give up runs so easily in baseball even when you have the best stuff you ever had. With the stakes so high, I had to keep my emotions in check and get us out of the inning.

Maintaining self-control lacks the dramatic flair of Shadrach, Meshach, and Abednego, but it is the place where the battle for purity is won or lost. The book of Proverbs says a man without self-control is as defenseless as a city with broken-down walls. That means when you lose your focus, when you lose your control, you're sunk.

I experienced this when I made my first World Series start in 1996 in Game 1 against the Atlanta Braves. Even though the

Yankees have won more championships than any other team in any sport, the franchise hadn't played in the series in fifteen years, and hadn't won one in eighteen. And here I was, coming off only my second season in the major leagues, and Joe handed me the ball to start the first game. I ended up giving up six or seven runs and only lasting two and a third innings. It was a situation where I let all of the expectations get to me and I lost my focus. Instead of thinking about pitching I was thinking, *Oh my gosh, it's Game 1 of the World Series, and I just gave up three runs in the second inning. This game is over.* I didn't make the same mistake again when I got the start in Game 5. I regained my focus and control and pitched one of the best games of my career, earning a 1–0 win against John Smoltz.

You have to be consistent in your walk with Christ and you have to stay in control. At some point in time you will find yourself in a situation that will push you to your limit. Remember, God knew this was going to happen long before you were born. He's not surprised by anything. When I'm pitching I try to keep my focus on Him and the fact that He's in control. That's the only way I can keep my emotions in check and my focus on doing what has to be done. The same will work for you. Self-control really means living with God in control.

Speaking Out without Words

When your convictions about living for Christ become an everyday part of your life, then making the right choices in a moment of decision comes naturally. You stand out without even trying. That's what impresses me about Daniel when he defied the king and was thrown into a den of lions. He took a stand by simply doing what he always did. Even though the king issued a decree saying everyone in the kingdom should pray to the king as if he were some kind of god, Daniel kept right on praying to the one true God just like always. The thing is, he wasn't trying to be different. He was simply being consistent. And his consistency made him stand out.

To last, the commitment you make to purity needs to grow into this same sort of lifelong conviction. For me, it's not enough that I stay out of the bars after games or avoid the women who throw themselves at professional athletes. My life needs to show my commitment to my God and to my wife and family. I love Laura more than anything. I pray for her every day, and I pray for our marriage that God will keep it strong and allow us to grow closer to each other and closer to Him. That's what I want the people around me to see. A couple of my friends I grew up with have told my wife they envy me. They don't envy me because I am a ballplayer, but because of my family and the relationship I have with my wife and kids. That's what purity is really about.

When your convictions become a daily part of your life, you sometimes end up taking stands without even knowing it. During my nine seasons with the Yankees, we won seven division titles, went to the play-offs as a wild-card team twice, took six American League pennants, and won four World Series titles. In all we won sixteen postseason series in those nine years, which means we did a lot of celebrating in the clubhouse. The team supplies several cases of champagne for celebrations, but the guys always spray more than they drink. Now I don't like champagne. One of my personal convictions is I don't drink, nor do I want to have any part of it. So instead of pouring champagne on my teammates, I usually grab a few water bottles and use them instead. It's not something I've ever made a big deal about. In fact, I've never really even given it much thought.

After we won the 2003 American League Championship Series against Boston on Aaron Boone's home run in the bottom of the eleventh inning, I ran into the clubhouse to celebrate with the team. We'd worked hard all year, and the Boston series was a hard fought victory. I was excited and I was excited for the team. As I walked into the clubhouse the team had a guy standing at the door handing out champagne. Usually they just have cases of the stuff placed around the room, but as I walked by the clubhouse attendant he handed me a bottle. I didn't want to embarrass the guy by saying something like, "No thanks, I don't drink," so I politely took it and kept going. I sat it down a few steps later and joined in the celebration.

I never thought anything about it until my cousin called me later that night. Apparently the Fox television cameras were following me, and they showed the whole incident on national television. My cousin, a youth pastor in Wichita Falls, Texas, told me how proud he was of me for being a role model and a strong Christian witness. My brother-in-law, a youth pastor in Big Spring, Texas, called the next day. His church members were calling him saying, "Can you believe what Andy just did!?" The calls just kept coming, all of them thanking me for the stand I took in the clubhouse.

To me, the whole thing was no big deal. I wasn't out to take a stand against alcohol. I was just living out my convictions, and God arranged it where people noticed. The camera could have just as easily cut away after the attendant handed me the bottle, which would have left people with a completely different impression altogether. I wasn't trying to stick out as different, nor was I trying to give anyone the impression I think I am better than they are. But it is like I said before. When you try to honor Christ with every part of your life, you will be different.

Taking a Stand

I'm not the most vocal person in the world. Usually I prefer to let my life speak for me. But there are times all of us will have to speak out. This goes hand in hand with living a consistent life for Christ. If you aren't consistent, if you don't live out your convictions and exercise self-control, no one will listen if you try to speak out. But there comes a point when a silent witness isn't enough. You have to stand up for what is right.

I found myself in that situation several years ago. My oldest son, Josh, was about four or five years old at the time. After one of our games, I took him into the clubhouse so he could use the bathroom. As we walked into a stall there was a pornographic magazine lying wide open. I glanced down and there was the nastiest pictures you can imagine, and my son was standing there looking right at it! Pornography in the clubhouse was nothing new. When I find it laying around I just kick it out of my way because I don't want to see it. But this was different. My little boy had just been exposed to pictures no one should ever see. And I just about lost it.

Immediately I went to the clubhouse attendant and told him I didn't appreciate having this stuff laying around and that I wanted it cleaned up and put out of sight. He told me there was nothing he could do since there were guys on the team who wanted it. So I went to them and confronted them about it. But I didn't threaten them or yell or anything like that. Nor did I demand they remove all pornography from the clubhouse. I didn't feel like I had the right to tell them they couldn't have that stuff in the clubhouse anymore than they could tell me I couldn't have a Bible study before batting practice. Instead, I went to them and explained the situation. And they listened. Afterward, instead of leaving objectionable material laying around, they locked it away when they weren't reading it.

There comes a point when you strive to live a life of purity that you have to take public stands. You not only have to live out your convictions, you have to stand up for them as well. In this situation, I knew I needed to do something because it was affecting my kids, not only me. I've found that when you stand on your beliefs, people respect you for it. People appreciate someone who shows they have a backbone.

When you stand up for what you believe, some guys will make smart-alecky comments about you. But that's probably because they are jealous of you. They wish they could be as strong and stand up for what they believe. Going along with the crowd is easy. Taking a stand takes real courage. And remember, simply making the commitment to a life of purity sets you apart. Your choice causes you to take a stand, even though it may not feel like it.

Study Questions

- Convictions drive us to do what is right *no matter what*. Have you ever faced a situation when you needed to take a stand and do what was right even though no one else was willing to do so? How was your stand tested? What was the end result?
- The last question assumes you did the right thing and took a strong stand on the truth. That's not always the case. Have you ever needed to take a stand but you didn't? What excuses did you make to yourself and God to justify your actions? If you could rewind life and do things differently, what steps would you take? Life doesn't rewind, but it is safe to say you will probably face a similar test in the near future. What will you do today to prepare yourself for a better outcome?
- Most of the stands you will have to take will lack the dramatic flair of Daniel or Shadrach, Meshach, and Abednego. Andy says consistency in our daily walk and self-control is the place where the battle for purity is won or lost. What is the relationship between daily consistency and taking a public stand for Christ? Can you have one without the other? The answer to that last question is pretty obvious, so let's take it a step further. What connection do you see between the two in your life? How are you doing with both? How can you improve?

- Read Daniel 3:1–26. Then read Hebrews 11:36–40. God saved Shadrach, Meshach, and Abednego from the fire, but Hebrews reminds us that doesn't always happen. Sometimes taking a stand doesn't have a happy ending. Andy told the story about taking a stand against pornography in the team clubhouse. His story ended well, but it could have just as easily blown up in his face. If it had, would he have been better off to simply ignore the magazine and not risk creating friction on the team? Why or why not? If Andy's teammates had not responded favorably, would taking a stand still be worth it? Why or why not? This isn't just a discussion about Andy Pettitte. You never know how people will respond when you take a stand. Are you prepared for both a good and a bad outcome? How?

Priceless

CHAPTER EIGHT

Why Should I "Just Say No" and Miss All the Fun?

BOB

Why am I challenging you to say no to premarital sex? Because I want you to enjoy fifty years of great sex! But I want you to do it in the way God intended it—in the boundaries of marriage!"

Those words are from my friend, Neal Jeffrey. Before playing in the NFL, Neal was a nationally renowned quarterback at Baylor University. Today he serves as the head of all student ministries at Prestonwood Baptist Church in Dallas. He has a great relationship with the students, and they know he's always looking out for their best interests, including their sex lives. Neal makes it clear that God has a plan for sex that leads to our maximum enjoyment of it. Let me say it again. *God really wants you to have a great sex life! That's why He designed such a great plan.*

His plan goes back to the beginning. Genesis tells us that when God created Adam, He gave him the run of the most amazing space a guy could ever have. It was flawless, but while Adam had everything he needed, he was lonely. That's when God made the greatest creation of all. He made a woman to be the absolutely perfect complement to a man. His plans were for a man and a woman to leave their parents and join together as a couple, becoming one in a covenant before God. And God's plans never changed! It's *only* within that boundary that God intends sex to take place.

But What about Today's Culture?

We can see that most people in our culture aren't buying into God's plan. They think they've got a better one, one that looks something like this:

If you want satisfaction in life, then go after every thrill and grab every experience. And there's no thrilling experience that feels as good, brings as much rush, or is as much fun as sex!

Sex is one of the most emotionally explosive experiences humans can have. Any guy who wants to experience this to the fullest must first understand how God meant things to be. Let's look at several issues that are a challenge for guys.

"I Can't Keep My Hands Off of Her"

Brad had been dating Stephanie for months. Both came from Christian families and had good reputations at school and church. At first their times alone seemed unintentional, but soon they became more physically intimate, finding more and more excuses to be alone—in a car or at one of their houses. Holding hands evolved to embraces. Embraces advanced to kissing—and then French kissing. Soon Brad's hands began to explore outside of Stephanie's clothes. It seemed so natural and so right. Stephanie let it go on, despite her confusion. Deep inside she knew it wasn't right, but the attention felt so good. Her dad, the other guy in her life, worked hard and traveled so often that she barely saw him. It felt great to have a male give her attention and make her feel loved and wanted. So she let Brad's hands move from outside to inside her clothing. Brad wanted the same kind of stimulation from her. It wasn't long before this Christian couple hurtled toward an emotional cliff.

What every guy must understand is that Brad's actions are what in the proper context of marriage is called *foreplay*. Husbands and wives caress each other in areas loaded with nerve endings that bring rapid and exciting stimulation. But foreplay is meant for only one thing—to lead to fulfillment in sexual intercourse. It's part of—but *only* part of—how a man and a woman within the gift of marriage express their love physically for each other based on a commitment they've already made spiritually and emotionally. God's intention was never for foreplay to become an experiment outside the bounds of marriage.

So what's a guy to do? The answer is pretty simple and straightforward. Keep your hands outside of her clothes, and definitely keep them away from areas the underwear covers!

"But We're Not Really Having Sex . . ."

Sean and Brittany struggled with their justifications of covering what, deep inside, they knew they shouldn't be doing. They once were active in church but eventually drifted away, feeling uncomfortable because of their private lives. Making out led to more than what they'd anticipated. Sean and Brittany committed to each other to hold off on sex until they got married, but that didn't stop them from getting physically involved with each other to the point of mutual masturbation. The confusion was they found it to be exciting but, at the same time, frustrating. They became impatient and critical of each other. The relationship that was supposed to be so great, instead, grated on them. It became harder and harder to convince themselves they weren't having sex.

Why? It's because nowhere in God's plan is sex limited

strictly to the act of intercourse. Sexual activity that's a substitution for intercourse always leads to frustration, a sense of emptiness, and a lot of confusion and shame. That's the way God wired it. What Sean and Brittany both needed to understand is that in God's eyes they were *deeply* involved in sexual immorality. In 1 Corinthians 6:13 God says, "The body is not for sexual immorality but for the Lord, and the Lord for the body." When God refers to the term *immorality* in Scripture, He definitely includes the kind of activities in which Sean and Brittany are involved. He doesn't see it as "experimenting" or as "stopping short," and He definitely doesn't see it as "*not* having sex." *Nowhere* in Scripture will you find any biblical guidelines that allow for such justification and warped perspective.

We can't continue without addressing the issue of oral sex. A trend is sweeping the country, even into junior high. It's referred to as "giving a Monica" or "Clintoning." Both terms exist because of the tragic example set by our former president, Bill Clinton. When accused of having oral sex with White House intern Monica Lewinsky, he publicly declared that *he did not have sex with that woman.* How could he say that?! Because to Mr. Clinton, anything short of intercourse with a woman was "not having sex." He never clearly declared what sex was—only what *he believed* it wasn't.

But this same warped perspective can be seen in a growing trend among young people called "technical virginity." People fool themselves into thinking that if they refrain from intercourse, they remain virgins, even if they engage in a variety of other sexual activity. But this is nothing more than a word game that can lead to tragic consequences. As I've already mentioned, the Bible uses the same word to describe every kind of sensual behavior outside the realm of marriage: *immorality.* That means foreplay is sex. Oral sex is sex. Mutual masturbation is sex. And, of course, intercourse is sex. All sexual activity outside of the realm of marriage is not only sin; it also carries the same risks of disease along with taking an emotional toll.

One thing that anyone with half a brain can understand is that you can't play with fire and walk away without getting burned. You also can't play both sides against the middle with God without getting squeezed in the process.

- "Let us fix our eyes on Jesus, the author and perfecter of our faith" (Hebrews 12:2 NIV). It's *impossible* to keep your focus on Jesus Christ and flirt with sex at the same time.

- "Whatever is true, whatever is honorable, whatever is just, whatever is pure, whatever is lovely, whatever is commendable—if there is any moral excellence and if there is any praise—dwell on these things" (Philippians 4:8). Involvement in sexual activity (including Internet porn) outside of marriage undermines "honorable and pure" thoughts.

- Paul counseled young Timothy: "You should be an example to the believers in speech, in conduct, in love, in faith, in purity" (1 Timothy 4:12). Involvement—mentally or physically—in sexual activity outside marriage will make you into an example, for sure—a WRONG example!

"But I'm Being Careful . . ."

Sam came to me frustrated and confused. He and his girlfriend of one year had been having sex on and off for the last five months. But what he thought would be a great experience for him and Lisa had turned out to be anything but. She was agitated and irritable more often than she was loving and caring. Sam felt frustrated with her, and they were fighting a lot. While Lisa claimed what they were doing was wrong, Sam argued it was acceptable because they were being careful. In other words, he was using a condom.

While advertisements claim that condoms are great protection, there is information missing from the manufacturers who make such claims. *No condom is absolutely predictable.* Many pregnancies occur when condoms are used. Besides that, condoms aren't consistently effective against sexually transmitted diseases. *There is NO guaranteed protection in intimate relationships—except abstinence!* Condoms also can't protect anyone from the guilt of doing what their gut instincts tell them is wrong. Guilt goes with you wherever you are. It doesn't take vacations, leaves of absence, or breaks.

And what about shame? Oh, it's easy to say you love her and will marry her, but what happens when you don't? Or what happens when the condom fails and you have to step up to the responsibility of an unwanted pregnancy? How about the responsibility of being a dad way before your time? What will happen to school? How about never being able to get a well-paying job? What will you tell your parents? And what about her parents?

The worst part may be the memories that will be etched in your mind forever. It's amazing how many divorces I'm familiar with in which the husband and the wife had premarital sex. They tell me that when they tried to make love with their mates, they would continue to relive sexual escapades they had with others before marriage. The results ranged from guilt to shame to comparison to disgust and even to impotence. Does that sound like a good future? Does that sound like what a loving God had in mind when He designed sex?

So What's a Guy to Do?

With temptation coming from every direction and so many voices calling, "Try it, you'll like it!" what's a guy to do? Remember that God promised He would not allow temptation to be so overpowering that you can't handle it. He promised that He would *always* provide a way of escape. The question is this: Are we looking for the escape route, and when we see it, do we use it?

Personally, I've found no better guidance than James 4:7–10: "Therefore, submit to God. But resist the Devil, and he will flee from you. Draw near to God, and He will draw near to you. Cleanse your hands, sinners, and purify your hearts, double-minded people! Be miserable and mourn and weep. Your laughter must change to mourning and your joy to sorrow. Humble yourselves before the Lord, and He will exalt you." In this passage, God gives specific steps for keeping your life on track in the area of sexual purity.

Submit Yourselves to God

Here the direction is to make sure that there's no area of your life in which God does not have control, including your dating life and sexual life. It means you should regularly pray for God to give you the strength to resist temptation, the awareness to recognize it when it knocks, and the will to say no until in marriage.

How are you doing in that area? Have you kept God out of any areas in your dating life? Would you be embarrassed if He were watching any of your activities? If so, just remember . . . HE IS! By the way, don't forget that submission to God includes your thought life as well as your physical actions. It's not one or the other—it's both.

Resist the Devil, and He Will Flee from You

Resisting takes an act of the will. It is a determination to *not do something* and to *not give in to temptation.* To resist requires a force reacting to the pressures you face. And resistance best happens when you've made up your mind to resist before an opportunity to compromise ever arrives. The time to determine what you'll do in the backseat of a car or in an empty house with a girlfriend is before you get into either situation. That's the thing that will keep you protected and guarded.

Draw Close to God, and God Will Draw Close to You

This also is an act of the will. It means that you're cultivating your spiritual relationship with God and keeping the fire of your love for Him stoked. You're not trying to find how close to the edge of sexual impurity you can walk and still have the reputation of being a Christian. Instead, what you're doing is growing more in love with Christ so that you're determined to do *nothing* that would grieve Him about your actions and thoughts. This counsel can best be summed up in a simple quote my pastor often uses, *Stay close and you'll stay clean!*

The Consequences Can be Fatal

Remember King David? In 2 Samuel 11, we find David in the wrong place at the wrong time. Instead of being with his troops on the battlefield, he's on the palace roof watching a naked woman bathe. And what happens when *any of us* aren't where we should be and end up being where we shouldn't? Trouble is usually just around the corner.

The story unfolds as David asks about the identity of the beautiful woman. He learns she's the wife of one of his chief officers. Throwing caution to the wind and disregarding God's clear directives to him about purity and obedience, he sends for the woman. They end up spending the night together, and he thinks that one-night stand will be the end of the relationship. But the Bible tells us that we reap what we sow (Galatians 6:7–8).

And so it was with David. When he learned that Bathsheba was pregnant, he immediately began to backpedal and cover up. That attempt led him to lie, manipulate, and even commit murder. Remember what Galatians 6 said? "The one who sows to his flesh will reap corruption from the flesh, but the one who sows to the Spirit will reap eternal life from the Spirit." It doesn't mean merely "physical death," like the murder of Bathsheba's husband Uriah, which was ordered by David. Other things die too—like our purity, our conscience, our integrity, our spirituality, and our sensitivity.

David continued trying to cover up and justify his wrong-doing for almost a year. When he couldn't stand the guilt, the shame, and the convicting hand of God in his life any longer, he finally came clean. You'll find his prayers of confession in Psalm 32 and Psalm 51. He describes how miserable he was while trying to cover up what he did. What he thought would be exhilarating, satisfying, fulfilling, and enjoyable turned into misery, conviction, embarrassment, and consequences that would last a lifetime. And the consequences affected everyone around him with tragedy after tragedy.

David was so human, which is why we can learn from him. The lyrics to his songs (the Psalms) show he was depressed at times. David seems like the least likely person to become depressed until you consider his adultery with Bathsheba. He'd proven his strength and manhood by defeating Goliath. He'd become a rich and powerful king. And get this: he had such a close walk with the Lord that he was known as "the man after God's own heart." Yet David strayed. And the complications from David's sin led to more than heartache. They led to depression.

Thousands of years after David lived, people still experience depression. A report that came out in 2003 concludes that sexually active teenagers are more likely to be depressed and to attempt suicide.[10] Read the sobering conclusions of the report:

- Guys who are sexually active are more than *twice as likely* to be depressed as those who are not sexually active.

- Sexually active teenage guys are *eight times more likely* to attempt suicide than guys who aren't sexually active.

- When asked "If you have had sexual intercourse, do you wish you had waited longer?" of those who said they had engaged in sexual intercourse, *nearly two-thirds stated that they wished they had waited longer before becoming sexually active.*

- More than half of sexually active guys and nearly three-quarters of sexually active girls regard their own initial sexual experience unfavorably—as an event they wish they had avoided.
- The most likely explanation of the overall link between teen sexual activity and depression is that early sexual activity leads to emotional stress and reduces teen happiness.

What If We Blow It?

We're like David. If we commit a sin in our lives where we've knowingly crossed the line given to us by God for our own good, we learn that the sin never affects just us. *We always get others involved whether we like it or not.*

James 4 tells us that if we've blown it, we must repent, admit we're wrong, and have a broken heart over what we've done. Merely saying "I'm sorry" doesn't come close to what God requires. When that's all we're willing to say, the only thing we're usually sorry for is getting caught or facing the consequences. We're not sorry about breaking the heart of God and rupturing our fellowship with Him. And that's what He's looking for.

So if you've blown it, you can be restored as David eventually was restored, but only after a lot of grief and a huge cost. God can forgive your sin and remove it as far as the east is from the west (Psalm 103:12). He is willing to give you a brand-new beginning. However, it would be unfair for me to leave it there. Even with the forgiveness of God and a brand-new fresh start, *there will be consequences.* Don't misinterpret grace. Sin doesn't come without a price, and the price can be significant.

Now, listen to the promise: "Humble yourselves before the Lord, and He will exalt you" (James 4:10). Now that may be one of the greatest promises you'll ever hear in a lifetime. So if you need it, be sure to take advantage of it right now.

Worth the Wait

ANDY

W hen I was a kid playing baseball in my hometown of Deer Park, Texas, I dreamed of someday making it to the big leagues. After signing with the Yankees and working my way through the minors, that was still my dream. But once I made it I wanted so much more. Every ballplayer dreams of winning championships, and as a pitcher, you cannot imagine anything more awesome than the possibility of standing on the mound for Game 7 and helping your team win the World Series. You want to be your best when the games mean the most.

The games never meant more to me or to my team than they did during the 2003 postseason. Our team had the best record in the American League, which meant every series started in Yankee Stadium. Yet, in all three series of the play-offs, we lost the opening game. That made Game 2 a must-win. In all three series, Joe Torre handed me the ball to make the start. I got a taste of playing under this kind of pressure in my second year in the majors when I started Game 1 of the 1996 World Series. I don't know if I really appreciated the full weight of it at the time. I did in October 2003.

I'm not trying to sound arrogant, but I have to say, walking out to the pitcher's mound to start a game we absolutely had to win is the ultimate for me. This made all the work through the minor leagues and running all those miles during the season and doing all those sit-ups and lifting all the weights worth it. I've strived my entire career to be in this position. I love having to be my absolute best on the big stage of October. I felt like the team had a lot of confidence when our backs were against the wall with me pitching, and that gave me even more confidence. Before I walked onto the field I prayed and put the whole thing in God's hands. What happened after that was the ultimate for me as an athlete. I pitched the games of my life, and the Yankees won every one of my Game 2 starts.

The best moment of the 2003 postseason, probably the best moment of my career individually, came in the late innings of Game 2 of the World Series against the Florida Marlins. I'd pitched a really good game and helped the Yankees win a game we had to have. Then, in the eighth and ninth innings, the sell-out crowd at Yankees Stadium started chanting my name. Nothing like that had ever happened for me in my nine seasons in New York. I don't know if the fans just wanted to show their appreciation for all I'd done in my career because they thought I might be leaving the team soon, but this was one of my greatest moments in baseball. I don't care about recognition, and I've never been a guy who needed to be in the headlines. But to have the fans show that kind of love for me was absolutely amazing. All the work, everything I'd done my entire life as a ballplayer, was suddenly worth the effort.

God's Best

Throughout this book, Bob and I have tried to show purity as a commitment to honor God with every part of your life. A lot of the discussion has centered around sex because that is one of the primary areas in your life Satan loves to attack. Resisting his assaults and keeping your commitment won't be easy, but I can guarantee you, it will be worth the effort. The payoff is more than standing at the altar on your wedding day knowing you've put off sex until you were married. If it were all you had to look forward to, that would make this whole thing sound like nothing but one big negative. Nothing could be farther from the truth. When God gives us commands, He doesn't just tell us *not* to do something. He loves us, and He is always looking out for our best interests. When God says to avoid something bad, it is because He always has something better waiting for us.

And when it comes to sex, God does have something better for you. He wants you to someday enjoy a relationship with your future wife that will be better than anything you can imagine. After all, God created marriage. Shortly after He made the first man, He took part of the man's side and formed it into a woman. God knew the man was incomplete without her. He then presented the first woman to the first man and gave them to each other. You might say God performed the first wedding ceremony. The Bible then says, "This is why a man leaves his father and mother and bonds with his wife, and they become one flesh" (Genesis 2:24).

Here's what I find amazing about this story. God picked out Adam and Eve for each other. The Bible goes on to tell us God has a plan for each of our lives, and that plan includes your future spouse. When you make a commitment to purity, you aren't just saying no to sex until you are married. Instead you are committing yourself right now to that special girl God has picked out for you to marry someday. You aren't just waiting for sex. You are waiting for her.

This was how Laura and I thought of our commitments before we were married. Laura committed herself to purity when she was a girl, long before we even met. Even at a young age she vowed to save herself for the one God had for her. The older she got, the stronger her commitment became. She wanted her first time to be on her wedding night with the man she knew God had picked out for her. Until that day arrived, she wouldn't allow anything to spoil that special moment for her. She also wanted the man she married to share her conviction, which I did. In a very real sense, Laura and I saved ourselves for each other.

I cannot tell you how special her commitment made me feel. She hadn't just promised God she would stay pure. It was as though she had committed herself to me even before she knew me, and long before we stood at the altar and said, "I do." Purity was a commitment she made to God for me. This only made me love her even more when we got married. You may not be able to understand this fully, and it is really hard to explain, but when you start to look at the spiritual side of a relationship like this, it makes your love grow deeper and stronger.

This is how God wants a marriage to begin. Laura and I didn't start off with a load of guilt from past mistakes. Nor did we have to overcome the memories and distrust which come when people have sex with other people before they are married. By God's grace we were able to start off with a clean slate and totally commit our home to the Lord, and I know Bob and his wife, Cheryl, made this same commitment. When Laura and I stood before God and made vows to Him and each other, we started our marriage in the direction we knew He wanted us to go. The promises we made when we said "I do" were really extensions of the commitments we'd made to the Lord. As I look back on our twelve years of marriage, I see how God has blessed us as a result.

Friends for Life

The payoff on purity goes beyond the moment of standing at the altar. Good marriages start out as strong friendships. During the six years Laura and I dated we became each other's best friend. We were in love and we knew we were going to get married. But we also knew that sex wasn't going to happen until we were married, which gave us the freedom to stop worrying about it. Instead, we were able to develop the kind of friendship that has continued to grow stronger the longer we are married.

My lifestyle made this all a little crazy. Once I signed with the Yankees, Laura and I hardly saw each other. During the season I was moving around through the minors, then during the off-season I played in the Yankees' instructional leagues. We rarely had the opportunity to spend any time together. We settled for hours and hours talking on the phone. She was the only person I really wanted to talk to while I was away from home, especially when God did things in my life. My whole goal in the minor leagues was the same as my goal now. More than anything I wanted to live a life that honored the Lord. When God used my testimony to talk to someone about Him, I immediately wanted to call Laura and tell her all about it. Once we finally got married, our friendship moved to a whole new level.

I can't tell you enough how important this is, and how this ties in directly to your commitment to sexual purity. Too many couples get so focused on the physical part of their relationship that they never develop a strong friendship. Then, once they do get married, they find they aren't prepared for the demands of marriage. The thrill doesn't last because they did everything they could do before they got married. They didn't leave themselves anything to look forward to. But beyond that, they didn't take the time to really get to know each other, to build the kind of friendship that grows stronger with time.

Spiritual Oneness

The relationship God wants you to have with your future wife starts with friendship, but it doesn't end there. It builds on love and romance, but they are not all you need. A home built on God is a place where you and your spouse grow closer to each other spiritually. Think of a marriage as a triangle, with God at the top and you and your spouse on the sides. The closer you both grow to God, the closer you grow to each other.

This is where God takes your relationship to levels you never thought possible. His plan is for you and your spouse to help each other grow closer to Him. That's how Laura and I are. I feel like every year we've grown a little more in different areas of our lives. We're able to talk about our struggles and pray for each other. When she's struggling with something I pray for her, and she does the same for me. No one likes to wrestle with anything, yet God uses trials to make us grow up in our faith. And when a marriage is built on Him, the two of you grow together.

In an earlier chapter I mentioned the four-game losing streak I had during the 2003 season. The night I lost the fourth game—a blowout loss to the Toronto Blue Jays—I came home at the end of my rope. I fell into bed completely stressed out. Laura and I talked a little bit, but soon she started singing a song to me called "Let It Fall." The song talks about leaving everything in God's hands and letting it all fall into place. God spoke through my wife as she sang. For me, this was the turning point for my season. I told God that I was going to stop trying to do everything on my own. That night I stopped worrying about how I needed to be great and about my record. Instead I started relying on God to get me through. At the time my record was 4–5. I finished the year by winning seventeen games and losing only three for a record of 21–8. God turned everything around, and He used my wife to do it.

Marriage is about so much more than physical intimacy. The closeness you feel goes beyond anything you can imagine. That's why purity is worth the price. Doing things God's way always is.

More than You Can Imagine

I loved my wife when we got married, there's no doubt about it. But, the longer we're married, the more my love for her grows. Laura is, to me, the very picture of what the Bible says a wife is to be. Ephesians 5:22–26 gives God's blueprint for marriage: "Wives, submit to your own husbands as to the Lord, for the husband is head of the wife as also Christ is head of the church. He is the Savior of the body. Now as the church submits to Christ, so wives should [submit] to their husbands in everything. Husbands, love your wives, just as also Christ loved the church and gave Himself for her, to make her holy, cleansing her in the washing of water by the word." This is exactly how Laura lives. She isn't under me or beneath me as though she were somehow inferior, but she is submissive to me as her husband. In every home someone has to make the final decisions, and the Bible lays that responsibility on the husband. My wife supports me in this. She sticks with me no matter what the situation may be. As I watch how she cares for me and our family out of love, and how she never complains about the ups and downs of this crazy life my career brings on our family, I can't help but love her more and more. I love her so much that I want to give back to her. My goal is to give her the best I possibly can.

God doesn't just want to bless Andy Pettitte with this kind of marriage. This is His plan for every one of His children. That's why purity is worth the sacrifices you make now. Sure, you have to tell your flesh no even when it doesn't want to hear it. But don't ever lose sight of why you are doing this. You aren't just denying yourself something that you really want. Instead, when you live your life the way God wants you to live it, you are putting yourself in a position to experience His blessings. That doesn't mean you will have a perfect marriage if you commit yourself to purity before you are married. That's not what I am saying. But I am telling you that if you do things God's way, life is much, much easier.

Final Encouragement

I know keeping your commitment to purity isn't easy. But don't let the fact that this is difficult keep you from trying. No goal worth reaching will ever be handed to you. Everything worth doing takes a great deal of work. Purity is no different.

And never forget, I'm not the one telling you to keep yourself pure. This command doesn't come from your parents or your pastor or your youth leader. You might hear this message from all of them, but that's not where it starts. You should live a life of purity because God asks you to do it. He tells you and me to be holy because He is holy (1 Peter 1:16). If you claim to be a

Christian, if you want to be like Christ, this is the way you are supposed to live.

I hope you understand that God's commands aren't just negative. He wants to give you His full blessings and fill your life with joy. You can't expect Him to do this if you ignore what He says. I'm not saying that purity guarantees you won't have problems in your life. But, I believe a life of purity is biblical. This is the way God wants us to live. I believe when we try to honor Him with a right heart, He honors our efforts.

Study Questions

- What will living a life of purity cost you? Again, we aren't talking about the people Bob used as examples. Look at your own life. What will your commitment to purity cost you?
- What makes purity worth the price for you personally? Don't just focus on the negatives. Anyone can say they don't want to do drugs because they don't want to lose the brain cells, but is that really enough? What do you really want out of living a pure and holy life?
- Read 1 Peter 1:3–9. These verses remind us our faith, and our commitments, will always be tested to prove whether they are genuine. How has your commitment to purity been tested in the past, and how will it be tested from this point forward? Why keep it?
- Chapter 8 is called "Priceless." Is purity really priceless? Why or why not? The value we give things affects the way we treat them. What does the way you live your life say about the value of purity? Is this an accurate reflection of what you believe its value to be? Now what will you do?

The Wrap-Up

BOB

One hundred million of these are scattered across almost every continent on Earth. Another 100 million or more are stockpiled in countries all over the world. Every day, an average of seventy people are killed or injured by them—that's one person every fifteen minutes—twenty-six thousand every year. And, if you really want your heart ripped out, think of the three hundred thousand children who, because of their tragic missteps, were severely disabled during the few minutes you read the Wrap-Up chapter of this book.

What are we talking about? Land mines—exactly where we started in this book. Land mines can cost as little as three dollars to make, yet require more than a thousand dollars to locate and disarm. And while it may take only one hour to plant a land mine, it will take more than one *hundred* hours to diffuse and extract one after it's been found. They leave a devastating reminder for those who survive them. Of the 250,000 people around the world who became amputees due to tragic encounters with land mines, the cost to provide prostheses to compensate for their lost limbs is approximately $750 million![11]

Think of it. A land mine can explode, and an arm or leg is gone forever. That's tragic in the physical dimension where we live, but—whether we admit it or not—a far greater tragedy is the destruction to our spiritual lives when sin blows up in our faces. And just as physical land mines wreak havoc on physical bodies, the *spiritual land mines* Satan lays before us will devastate not only our futures but our souls if we blunder into them.

Remember this book's opening story about the men in Vietnam who, under the chaos of enemy fire, panicked and ran into a minefield? That was the enemy's whole intent, to confuse, unnerve, and drive them into an unpredictable action. It's one of the same strategies Satan uses with your life!

But don't forget the warning in chapter 4. Sometimes Satan simply lures you into "off-limit areas," making you think there's *something better just around the corner* or *something God's been keeping from you*. Satan is predictable, always using the same search-and-destroy tactics.

He'll lead you to question God. He'll make you wonder if God really does want what's best for you. He wants you to ask, "What's so bad about trying this just once, even though God says not to do it?" His favorite lines are, "What's the big deal?" and "Nobody will ever know!" and of course his most favorite, "Doesn't God want me to be happy?"

When Satan attacks, he always tries to get you to contradict God. He'll put thoughts in your head like, *Maybe this is a problem for everybody else, but not for me!* Satan wants nothing more than for you to think of God as a killjoy who wants to keep you from having fun. And of course, he always tries to convince you that you can handle any situation.

Satan's tactics have never changed. He will entice you to become your own god, just like he did Adam and Eve in the Garden of Eden. He'll give you false confidence and make you think you know what's best for you. Sometimes he even uses the Bible, but he twists it and tries to get you to use it only when it works for you. One of Satan's favorite deceptions has become the dominant view of our culture: the relativity of truth. He wants you to think of right and wrong as a personal choice based on the circumstances you face.

But here's the bottom line, whether we end up in the minefield of life by being driven into it or by being lured into it, either way it's devastatingly dangerous.

So How Do We Avoid the Minefields in the First Place?

We offer a few questions to keep handy as you're moving through life. These will help you avoid stepping into a situation that could leave you emotionally, spiritually, or physically wounded. Try on our questions for size when you're faced with taking a step into unfamiliar territory, and you're not sure what the ramifications could be. Or you're on the verge of taking a step, but something deep inside your gut warns you this could be a dangerous stroll. Or still worse, you've taken a dangerous step and you feel like you may have stepped into something that could explode if you don't diffuse it *fast*. When you find yourself in the middle of these situations, ask yourself:

1. Can I ask God to bless what I'm about to do?
2. If I were involved in this kind of activity and suddenly Jesus walked in, would I be embarrassed?
3. Would if be OK with me if everybody else did what I'm thinking of doing (my parents, my family, my teachers, my minister, and even my future wife)?
4. Would the action I'm considering make God smile with pleasure? Or break His heart?
5. If things went wrong, what's the worst that could happen, and how many people would it affect?

Throughout this book we've dealt straight up with you about life as it really is when it comes to building character and living with integrity. We've tried to send our message right over home plate like one of Andy's fastballs. Because we're on your side, rooting for you, we chose not to draw you off with curveballs or sucker you in with sliders. Instead, we attempted to place the ball right in the strike zone so you can step up to the plate and hit a grand slam with your life. Now, the choice is yours.

We leave you with this reminder. Second Chronicles 16:9 says, "The eyes of the LORD range throughout the earth to strengthen those whose hearts are fully committed to him" (NIV). And James 4:7–8 reminds each of us: "Submit yourselves, then, to God. Resist the devil, and he will flee from you. Come near to God and he will come near to you" (NIV).

So, you've got a choice. You'll either hold fast to God's promises, plus the challenges and principles we've presented in this book . . . or you'll find yourself staggering through land mine-strewn territory, knowing that your future could be shattered with the next unwise step (or maybe the one you've just taken). The choice is yours.

As for us, **we believe in you! And we're pulling for you to hit a grand slam!**

Acknowledgments

Helen Spore has been amazing at helping me with the transcription of this manuscript, and Carolyn Curtis has been invaluable at shaping and forging the manuscript to help me make my writing a laser-focused instrument dealing with these essential characteristics of living a life that counts.

Gary Terashita has been the best editor a writer could desire to have. Always encouraging and helping to achieve the best, he has been a great partner in a most enjoyable effort.

My coauthor, Andy Pettitte, who is the REAL DEAL! What you read about in this book, Andy is. While privileged to be a highly successful professional athlete, I have never seen Andy wear it on his sleeve. Instead, I've always seen him practice servant leadership by helping to build others up more than himself. That only happens when you are playing your life to the right audience: Jesus Christ. Thanks, Andy, for living what you write!

—Bob Reccord

To Mark Tabb, thank you so much for spending countless hours on the telephone and for so accurately putting my thoughts on paper. My contribution to this book would have never been written if not for you. You are amazing.

To the New York Yankees, much of the contents written in this book came from the experiences that I shared while wearing the Yankee uniform. Thanks for nine great years.

To Bob Reccord, whom I admire greatly. You have written many books, and I count it a privilege to coauthor this one with you.

To my three children and one on the way, I hope someday as you grow older that you will understand the contents in this book and will live pure Christian lives. More than a baseball legacy, this is what I want you to remember.

—Andy Pettitte

Notes

1. George Barna, *The Second Coming of the Church* (Nashville, Tenn.: Word Publishing, 1998), 23.

2. Ted Roberts, *Pure Desire* (Ventura, Calif.: Regal Publishers, 1999), 69.

3. Chuck Swindoll, *You and Your Child* (Nashville, Tenn.: Thomas Nelson Publishers, 1977), 33.

4. Fred Stoeker and Stephen Arterburn, *Every Young Man's Battle* (Colorado Springs, Colo.: Waterbrook, 2002), 41–42.

5. Ibid., 129.

6. Associated Press, 8 August 2003.

7. Suzanne Fields, "Listening to Elders and saying no; Cultural warrior," *Washington Times,* 15 July 1993, Commentary, G1.

8. Josh McDowell, *Beyond Belief to Convictions* (Wheaton, Ill.: Tyndale House, 2002), 22.

9. J. A. Walter, *Sacred Cows* (Grand Rapids, Mich.: Zondervan Publishing House, 1979), 41.

10. Robert E. Rector; Kirk A. Johnson, Ph.D.; and Lauren R. Noyes, Report, Heritage Center for Data Analysis, 2 June 2003 (The Heritage Foundation, 214 Massachusetts Ave. NE, Washington, D.C. 20002), www.heritage.org.

11. "Statistics on Land Mines," HindustanTimes.com.

TruthQuest™

www.TruthQuestBible.com

Get Deep. Get TruthQuest.